SAMUEL W. TAYLOR

ASPEN BOOKS

Taylor-made Tales:
© 1994 by Samuel W. Taylor
All rights reserved
Printed in the United States of America

No portion of this book may be reproduced in any form
without written permission from the publisher,
Aspen Books, 6211 South 380 West,
Murray, UT 84107

Library of Congress Cataloging-in-Publication Data

Taylor, Samuel Woolley
Taylor-made Tales

p.   cm.
ISBN 1-56236-216-X
1. Taylor, Samuel Woolley, 1907 - Childhood and youth
2. Authors, American - 20th Century - Biography
3. Mormons - Utah - Social life and customs
4. Family - Utah
I. Title.
PS3570.A954Z474 1994
833'.54—dc20
[B]   94-32168
                                       CIP

Cover design by Brian Bean
Cover illustration by Jim Madsen
Interior photographs used by permission

CONTENTS

Sam at home

INTRODUCTION

When the Lord spared Samuel Woolley Taylor from death in a World War II B-17 crash landing, he was, as usual, waxing visionary *and* purposeful—and exercising divine restraint, as well. At first glance one might think he spared Sam's life in partial recompense for the trouble he had occasioned for Sam's grandfather, Mormon Prophet John Taylor, and for his father, Apostle John W. Taylor, and his mother, Nettie (not to slight May, Nellie, Roxie, Rhoda, or Ellen), good people who had been loyal to "the Principle"—and had paid a stiff price.

But there was an even better reason for sparing the life of this young writer: when Samuel Woolley Taylor stepped unscathed from that burning airplane (it's all in Chapter Thirteen), he was as one born again and keenly sensitive to the fact that providence had spared his life for a purpose. That purpose was almost immediately suggested to the seasoned writer of hundreds of published stories and articles by none other than Hugh B. Brown, president of the British mission and later LDS apostle and counselor to President David O. McKay. Bewailing the dearth of any literature explaining Mormonism and the Mormon people to the "outside world" of the gentiles, President Brown sparked in Sam a call—to interpret the Mormon people and their history for the gentiles—the non-Mormons who had generally misunderstood the Mormons. At the same time he could undertake to separate the myth from the pith for the Mormon people themselves, since the Saints, somewhere along the way, had selectively forgotten some of their history and mythologized and thus skewed other portions of their story.

In sparing Sam, the Lord knew he would have to put up with Sam's salt-and-peppered language, twinkle-in-the-eye irreverence and damned-if-I won't ways. "Let it go," he must have thundered from Kolob with raised seraphic eyebrows. "After all, he's a destined blend of the feisty Woolleys and the headstrong Taylors." So the Lord has granted Sam a long and productive life and tolerated Sam's forthright, sometimes crusty, the-king-is-wearing-no-clothes honesty and his coffee-drinking (only medicinal, of course) nose-thumbings at Mormon—or anyone's—sacred cows or persons.

And, as this delightful volume and Sam Taylor's ten other volumes about the Mormons and Mormonism attest, the Lord was right (He always is!); it was all "for a wise and glorious purpose." Sam's books, published by national publishing houses, have been welcomed by non-Mormons as fascinating glimpses into little known chapters of Americana. They have been fascinated, even stirred, by the human face which Sam Taylor has put on the abstractions and labels which had for over a century diverted attention from the Mormons as good people with a dream; men and women with great faith in their God, their leaders, and in the kind of unified effort and hard work it takes to lay foundations under those dreams and build cities around their visions of Zion. Sam Taylor has made many friends for the Mormon people.

Among the Saints, Sam's books have also been widely read and frequently cited—after some sputterings. Latter-day Saints, accustomed to viewing their history through rose-colored lenses, brightly, have come to understand that, after all of his attention to discomfiting facts, Sam's variegated lenses not only clarify, adjust, and correct, but underscore and tout the remarkable accomplishments of the Mormon people, who are, as Maurine Whipple pointed out, human beings first, and "saints only by adoption," a well-meaning and visionary people who may have stumbled occasionally, but have managed to right themselves and keep on going toward the still-bright and cherished dreams of a latter-day Zion.

After relishing these memoirs of Samuel Woolley Taylor, readers who have just made his acquaintance will want to read (and old friends will want to return to) such volumes as *Heaven Knows Why!*, still the funniest Mormon novel to date (though Sam is pleased to note that competition is finally appearing); *Family Kingdom*, the charming story of Sam's father, John W. Taylor, father of three dozen children and husband to six wives, who was dropped from the Quorum of the Twelve and the Church for marrying plural wives after the Second Manifesto (Sam and brother Raymond eventually had him fully reinstated); *Nightfall at Nauvoo* and *The Rocky Mountain Empire*, carefully researched and reader-friendly histories which—like all of Sam's histories—read like novels, about the rise and fall of Nauvoo and the little-discussed era between the end of Mormon settlement in the Great Basin Kingdom and the modern period of international growth; *The Kingdom or Nothing: The Life of John Taylor, Militant Mormon*; and the recent *The John Taylor Papers*, in which Sam enables behind the scenes insights into John Taylor's resistance to the U.S. Government's drive (and internal pressures) to end polygamy and bring the Church to its knees. All of this from one who continued to write dozens of articles, stories and plays for a national audience. Some of those stories were transformed, by himself and others, into such Hollywood films as *Flubber* and *The Absent-minded Professor*, which was nominated for the Screenwriter's Annual Award as "the best written American Comedy of 1961."

And now providence has enabled this volume, in which Sam

tells how it all came to pass, recounting delicious recollections about an era long gone and largely forgotten, as those "who knew not Joseph" (and Brigham, Heber, Parley, Orson, John, and Wilford) rushed to displace fifty years of living under "the Principle" with fifty years of accommodation to mainstream America. Sam Taylor bridges these eras.

"Who would tell if I didn't?" he asks, tapping his unique heritage as one of the last born to a polygamous marriage in American territory (there is still a scattering of aging children who stem from plural marriages in the Mexican Colonies), for wonderful stories from a little known strand in the colorful fabric of western Americana. Taylor tells these stories spryly, wittily, memorably, and well, as only Sam can.

Let's face it, while the Lord was intervening, he also endowed this irrepressible Provo son with fiction-making vision—the facility of seeing dramatically and writing it tellingly. Not only does Sam envision and then enliven history through breathing new life into the dry bones of painstaking research, faded journals and dusty ledgers, but he is able to visualize, set, and polish the events of his and others' lives as pearls of great price and enduring value, wrested with skill and craftsmanship from the stuff of human life.

Hurrah for Samuel Woolley Taylor—or, given the obvious nudgings of providence in Sam's life and works—perhaps a modestly loud *Hallelujah!* of tabernacular proportions would be more appropriate. Did I just hear a Voice rumble "Amen?!"

Richard H. Cracroft
Brigham Young University
July 1994

CHAPTER 1

MY FATHER'S SIX WIDOWS

No kid who has learned by age three to lie to federal deputies, who has lived on the underground under an assumed name, who has no birth certificate and has always stayed on the alert like a jungle animal, can ever again be satisfied with childish make believe.

As one of three dozen kids in a polygamist family with six wives, this was my way of life. I loved it. I knew the heady thrill of living dangerously. I was taught that we were a special breed of cat. How wonderfully fortunate we were, to be born in "the Principle," among the very last to be blessed with this incomparable privilege. And while I was only eight when my father passed on, I remember still every single time we were together, and treasure the wonderful secret that I was his favorite child. Of course each one of us believed that. My father was quite a charmer.

My father's six wives were alternately among the elite of Deseret, each family living in its mansion, and then again on the underground under assumed names, hiding their children from federal deputies seeking evidence of unlawful cohabitation, a felony at the time. They were alternately rich when their husband struck it lucky, or taking in boarders in a mansion, taking in washinging or doing dressmaking in a basement, working at menial jobs to support their families when my father's fortunes failed.

Then when Father fell from grace for taking wives after the Church had abandoned the practice, his projects collapsed, swallowing my Aunt Nellie's mansion and millinery shop, Aunt Roxie's and Aunt Rhoda's farms, Mother's mansion and brick barn, and the Two-Step Ladder enterprise.

When Father died a few years later, there was never a more conservative family on earth than my mother's. Above all, we wanted security, savings, property, things we could count on. But again, did we? We have always seemed to be either succumbing to our heritage or reacting against it. It is there. We were all Gamblers Anonymous, suckers for the long shot, pigeons for the big chance, batting the bankroll to draw for the inside straight flush of life.

I don't think my mother's brood were ever children. The pressures upon a plural family were too great for that civilized luxury. We were babies, and, by the time our front baby teeth fell out, young adults. Even before my father's death, his wives ran their households like widows; their children assuming mature responsibilities. The women had to lean on the little ones, because under the best of circumstances the husband couldn't be expected to spend more than one-sixth of his time in any one household. With circumstances of the very worst—with fanatical harassment, not to mention my father's far-flung business promotions—the possibility for anything resembling normal family life simply did not exist.

My mother's mansion at 287 East, Second North Street was called the Donovan place. This was the name of a former owner, who had lost it in a poker game.

I have vivid memories of the Donovan place. I lived there from the time I was born until I was five. At the back porch my father held me in his arms and pointed out

Halley's Comet, which I understood as "Hay Leaves" Comet. Soon afterwards we were on the underground. At one time Father had one wife in Utah (May), one in Canada (Nellie), and three in Mexico (Roxie, Rhoda, and my mother, Janet Maria).

The underground left a lasting impression on my mother. She never again felt secure. She never again had enough bottled fruit in the basement, enough jams and jellies, enough clothing for herself and family. There, she had lived under the name of Nettie May; and to the end of her life she was known as Nettie M. Taylor.

And there were wheels within wheels. Though my father had been officially cast out (excommunicated for taking additional wives after the Manifesto) my mother knew that this actually wasn't so. Her husband had been "called" as a church duty, to step down from the Quorum of the Twelve in order that Reed Smoot might retain his seat in the U.S. Senate.

As evidence of this, my mother continued to receive the same amount monthly from Salt Lake that she had been getting while he was in full standing. Each month I bicycled down to the Farmers and Merchants Bank to deposit the check, with instructions to deliver it to Brother Olsen and nobody else.

And though my father had been called to step down "temporarily," it was forty years later and long after his death that he was restored to his former priesthood, office, and blessings as a member of the Twelve.

The first and last time all six of my father's wives met together was at his funeral. He had dedicated his life to the dream of the great patriarchal family.

May, the first wife—the official Mrs. John W. Taylor—

remained apart from the melodrama, in Los Angeles. So she had missed the excitement of the chase and all the fun.

Even before my father's death we lost the farms, the millinery shop, and the steam-heated barn that had constituted his grand plan to form a family industry during his final period of affluence. The collapse also swallowed my mother's mansion and Aunt Nellie's mansion. We were in the old Brimhall house in Provo during the final summer of my father's life, when he sat under our great apple tree, visited by hundreds of friends who came to say good-bye. And after he was gone there was nothing to hold the great family together. Each wife went her separate way with her own brood, while my father's dream ended, at least upon this earth.

The dispersal of his family after he was gone indicates that it never was really a family at all, but a group of related families that had been held together by his devoted zeal in spite of appalling practical difficulties.

It was not true in our case that the tensions in a plural family were caused by jealousies among the wives and jockeying for favor. Nor is it true that the basic situation of one man having children by several women was inherently repugnant. Polygamy has been practiced too many thousands of years for it to be called either unworkable or contrary to human nature. In our family there was jealousy among the wives at times, there was heartache and wounded vanity. But these were things that could be surmounted, and the necessity for them to live a dedicated life welded the wives together in achievement.

What broke our family apart were differences in regard to money and property. Mother's brick barn, we used to say, almost killed Aunt Rhoda, and understandably. Begun when Father was temporarily rich, it was finished after the collapse of his latest enterprise. At a time when the kids were barefoot, some wives taking in boarders and others taking in washing, we finished one of the most elegant barns in Provo, and certainly one of the very few with steam heat. To Father it was absolutely essential to his grand plan for family industry, but Aunt Rhoda, her farm gone, and now living in a basement, was simply unable to see the broad picture as he envisioned it. She just never got over Nettie's brick barn. The barn subsequently became an apartment house.

My mother, in turn, had an almost compulsive desire for security. She was careful, thrifty, cautious. Throughout her entire married life she tried to get my father to apportion his income on an equitable basis among the wives and to make each wife responsible for getting by and making do with her share. Under this arrangement she would have squirreled away the nest egg so desperately needed by one of her temperament. However, my father would have no part of this plan. This plan wasn't a family arrangement. In a family, it was share and share alike, one for all and all for one. When he had money, he settled all debts for each family, regardless of whether a wife was thrifty or extravagant.

In practice, Father's philosophy placed a premium upon improvidence and penalized thrift. It encouraged a wife to have the best for her own family and even to go into debt.

We each owned our own clothing; but that was the extent of it. Just about everything else could be taken away to relieve the common want, if necessity required. Each wife owned her own home in her own name. But when family finances reached dire straits, the homes went into the common pot. Twice Mother lost the best house in town: one in Farmington, and the big white brick house with the steam-heated barn in Provo.

In response to the difficulties of the situation, long before Father died, the wives had devised two kinds of money. There was family money, which came when Father struck it rich, which was used to square away accumulated debts, and to buy presents for one and all; and there was personal money, earned the hard way over a cook stove or a washboard. Personal money was never shared.

It is no coincidence that no one in my father's family grew up with the slightest leaning toward Socialism. We had lived it; once was enough. For example, my oldest brother, Joe, had a team of horses, purchased with his own money. When he got a ranch and needed the team there, it was a difficult matter securing it, because the team was useful to other branches of the family. An old letter from Joe, in Mother's files, says, "Tell them I've got to have my team here on the ranch. No ifs, ands, or buts about it." The letter significantly omitted what would seem to be the obvious point, that it was his team to do with as he wished. But what he stressed instead was that his need was imperative, greater than that of anyone else in the family.

Since things were owned by everyone, no one owned anything and no one was responsible. Joe was unhappy with the condition of the horses when he finally secured them. Feelings were continually being hurt about the abuse of property. And yet, the family wasn't close enough to air such things by frank discussion. We felt it was essential to maintain the facade of sweetness and light and harmony between the branches of the clan.

For this reason, it was impossible to hire members of another branch of the family and maintain good feelings. It was impossible to go into partnership with them. We tried, time and again. We really earned an "A" for effort. But if a half brother wasn't doing the work we couldn't fire him or discipline him, as could be done with a stranger, nor could we bawl him out as would have happened with a full brother. We just smoldered.

These were the tensions and pressures and irreconcilable obstacles that made my father's grand dream of the great patriarchal family a fond delusion.

However, our way of life with Father had a profound effect on our subsequent patterns. My mother's children—Joseph, Rachel, Ruth, Lillian, Deli, Raymond, Sam, and Paul—have consistently seemed to be either succumbing to the family heritage or reacting against it, but it is always there.

Raymond inherited Father's passion for thinking big. During the uranium boom, he didn't have a couple of claims; he had hundreds of them. He drove big cars; he hatched one scheme after another. He lived like a million-aire. When he was talking with Charley Steen, who had already struck it rich with uranium, Raymond said, "The only difference between you and me is that you've got your million, and I haven't."

Paul was most like Father in looks and temperament. Rachel was the conservative member, shrewd with invest-ments, careful. One of mother's responses was to become an incurable pack rat.

While Mormons are counseled to store enough food and supplies to last for a year or two, in case of calamity, my mother possibly carried this to extremes. She never went to a grocery store without buying an extra can or two to tuck away. She loved rummage sales and secondhand stores. Over time her cellar became jam-packed with food stuffs—

hundreds of bottles of fruit, dozens of cases of canned goods, a five-gallon crock of eggs in water glass that had been in storage for years.

Little by little she acquired enough shoes, dresses, night-gowns, coats, gloves, hosiery and underthings in the original packages to have stocked a store. Her accumulation of miscellaneous treasures eventually packed every closet, three attics, a chicken coop, four garages, and the outbuilding that later became my studio when I was a budding author. Her children, and the other wives' children knew that if there was anything they needed, anything at all, she had it.

Years after I married, on a trip back home to Utah I found that the concrete of her front steps had chipped with the frost of the previous winter. "Do you know of anyone doing construction work?" I asked. "I could fix that with just a little sand and cement."

"Let me look." She disappeared to one of her treasure troves and returned quickly with some cement and some sand, neatly sealed in fruit jars. Even I was surprised. If I had racked my brain I could not have conceived of two substances less likely for a little old lady to have tucked away.

No doubt her wildly uncertain existence as the wife of John W. Taylor created the pack rat mania. Just as a pessimist has been defined as someone who has to live with an optimist, so my mother and her family became models of caution, thrift, and conservatism from being dependent upon the spectacular fluctuations of my father's schemes and promotions. For a quarter of a century she was alternately rich or poor, but with nothing to count on for tomorrow. She was either a lady of position as the wife of a high Church official, or a fugitive on the underground, living under an assumed name and coaching her children in evasion and deception to protect her husband, who was in hot water about having too many wives.

While he was juggling fortunes with his gold mines in Mexico, timberlands in the United States, colonization projects in Canada, and reclamation deals in all three countries, her credit limit at the grocery store was ten dollars, which didn't provide much cushion for eight children. Then, when he fell from grace for taking wives after the Church had officially banned the practice, the glamour of his position was gone, his name lost its magic, and his projects collapsed. When he died, there was no more conservative family in Utah than my mother's family. Above all, we wanted security.

Or so it would seem. But perhaps some of our father's contagious excitement was in our blood and was not to be overturned by a few hard times. We knew what it was like to live dangerously and throughout our lives we seem to have been drawn to big ideas and risky ventures.

The death of my father left his enormous family in the classic situation leading to juvenile delinquency. But while he was gone, he was there. My mother never spanked me. Her sharpest rebuke when I got into mischief was to ask, "What would your father think of such conduct?"

The six wives remained firm in the faith, up in their tithes, with temple recommends. Ellen worked for Beneficial Life; Rhoda and Roxie worked at the LDS Primary Hospital. They were all temple workers. All six were beauties, and each had opportunities to marry again. But they had been the wives of the incomparable John W. Taylor, and where to find his equal?

CHAPTER 2

THE SECOND COMING OF SANTA CLAUS

Four of my father's six wives lived in Provo during my childhood, a fortunate situation for the swarm of Taylor

May   Nellie   Nettie

John W. Taylor

Roxie   Rhoda   Ellen

kids, who numbered three dozen. My mother was one of the four Provo wives. Upon entering "the Principle" (as plural marriage was always referred to at home), my mother had received a special endowment in the temple ceremony which no longer is bestowed since the practice has been set aside. In return, she felt she had been blessed with eight choice souls, of which I was the seventh. She taught us how fortunate we were to be among the very last privileged to live the *fulness* of the gospel, and Christmas was tangible evidence. Santa Claus came twice to us, instead of the one time he visited homes of unfortunate children whose fathers had only one wife.

The first Santa visited the individual families, while the second came for the entire clan. Each of my father's wives had her own home, her own family unit. My mother, the third wife, and Aunt Nellie, the second, each had a large brick mansion. Aunt Roxie and Aunt Rhoda, wives four and five, had adjoining fruit farms just east of the Provo cemetery. As a child I never met the first wife, Aunt May, nor the sixth, Aunt Ellen, who lived in Salt Lake. The four Provo families joined together in my father's fond concept of the patriarchal clan of Abraham, Isaac, and Jacob, on festive occasions such as his birthday, holidays, or outings, and particularly at Christmas.

The first Santa came on Christmas Eve. Of course we kids pretended to scoff at Santa, but down deep . . . we made every preparation for his arrival. Getting a tree meant a hard day's hike up Rock Canyon, then cutting, and lugging the tree home. It was always amazing how the scrubby little conifer became enormous in the parlor. My sisters, meanwhile, were popping corn, then stringing popcorn and cranberries along with red and green paper chains to decorate the tree. Candles were popular as tree lights, but my mother wouldn't allow such a fire hazard. Red apples and paper flowers took the place of decorations from the store, though we did add a few yards of old tinsel, carefully saved from year to year.

Before going to bed Christmas Eve, we hung up our stockings and laid out a supper for Santa, knowing he'd be hungry from his busy night. Then as we snuggled in bed upstairs, his deep voice sounded from below. "Have all the children been good this year, Nettie?"

"Oh yes, Santa."

"Then I'll leave something for every one, and a Merry Christmas to you all!"

When we crept downstairs before daylight, we found Santa had eaten his supper and filled the stockings—the once-a-year orange in the toe, hardtack, homemade divinity, Boston creams, fudge, and a popcorn ball. Under the tree we found things needed and appreciated—overalls, shirts, underwear, and shoes. In addition, there were always books, with a top or marbles for the boys and dolls for the girls.

The dolls were something special. When the girls were small, they got a new doll each year, and they wore it out. But at eight, the age of accountability, came baptism, confirmation, and the last doll—a doll with real hair, eyes that shut in sleep, and limbs with articulated joints. The last doll would be treasured, and each Christmas thereafter the girls would receive accoutrements—dresses, coats, a dollhouse, a cupboard, and muffin tins with tiny real pies baked in them. When my sister Deli saw her last doll with blonde hair and big blue eyes with real lashes, high in the Christmas tree, she shrieked with delight and scrambled up the tree for it. Fortunately there were no candles, or the crash of the tree might have burned the house down.

I don't recall my father ever being present at this early morning family Christmas. However, he died when I was eight, so my mother's turn may have come when I was too young to remember. His grand entrance later on Christmas day was Santa's second coming.

We were alerted to his approach by the yelling of children down the street, for John W. Taylor seemed to be a special friend of every kid in Provo. I was firmly convinced I was his favorite child; and I remember how, on occasion, *he* helped *me* mow the lawn, hoe the radishes, pick fruit at the farms. My mother knew in her secret heart that she was the favorite wife, as did each of the other five. Oh yes, he was a charmer; but he truly loved every one of us, and we loved him. So each year as the kids began yelling at his approach, we ran down the street to greet him. He had a flair for the dramatic and always made a grand entrance. He arrived once at the reins of a coach and four, the Concord stage bursting with kids, his foot on the brake as he tooled the matched bays, keeping one hand free to tip his hat to the ladies and wave to the men. He knew everyone in town. That stagecoach with its leather springs stood for years in our brick barn, a reminder of memorable Christmases past.

Another time he arrived with a buggy full of Navajo rugs, rugs that are still in service after more than half a century. We were wild with excitement the year he dashed into view on a sulky with bicycle wheels harnessed to a high-stepping racehorse. Though the horse's name was Tom Marchal, we were secretly convinced that this was a ringer name and that the horse really was the famous pacer, Dan Patch. Whatever his name, approaching cars spooked him, particularly at night, and Mother was deathly afraid to ride in the buggy behind him.

With my father's arrival in town on Christmas day, the Provo clan gathered, alternately meeting at my mother's and my Aunt Nellie's big house. While the four wives worked in the kitchen and pantry preparing dinner for the horde, all the brothers and sisters played games. We never called a sibling of another mother a "half" sister or brother, being exhorted, "Don't cut your brothers and sisters in half." However, there were differences in our relationships. It never occurred to us, for instance, to exchange Christmas presents except in the immediate family, nor would a sister wife discipline another's children.

Some of the games we played were Run Sheepie Run, London Bridge Is Falling Down, tag games, and the Hat Race. The older boys set up the entire affair for each young kid in turn. First, we were shown the treasures hidden under the hat: a pocket knife, marbles, or candy. The treasures were owned by the older boys, who never lost them in the end. Then, I lined up with my brothers, and at the signal raced around the house for the hat. Despite being the smallest in the race, I somehow reached the hat first, dived for it, and, as the hat was lifted at the last instant, clutched a double handful of cow manure. I never won the Hat Race again.

Inside, awaiting dinner, my father was the beaming audience as his children performed—elocution, piano pieces, or songs. I had practiced "Jesus Wants Me for a Sunbeam," but to my horror my brother Nephi (Rhoda's son) sang it just before my turn on stage. I fled to the barn and burst into tears. We never cried in my father's presence, as I'd previously learned when he simply picked me up and put my head under cold tap water. With a family of our size there had to be discipline or there would be chaos.

I was still in the barn when my father came in, sat on a box, and putting me on his knee, asked if I'd sing "Jesus Wants Me for a Sunbeam" just for him. I did so, and he

said he'd never heard it sung better. Then he said, "Your
mother is very proud of your beautiful hair." She brushed
the long curls each morning and fixed a topknot on the
crown of my head.

"But I look like a girl."

"And how old are you, Samuel?"

"Almost four."

"Old enough to be a little man." He drew a pair of
scissors from a pocket and proceeded to give me a haircut,
much to my delight.

When we went in and took our places at the table, my
mother said, "Where's Samuel?"

"Right here, Mama." We all laughed as she stared at the
shorn lamb.

"Well, John," she said, "and a Merry Christmas to you."

As we all sat around the table Christmas afternoon one
particular year, we had an unscheduled thrill. We were
singing my father's favorite hymn, "God Be With You,"
when Cliff put a clothespin on the tomcat's tail. The cat let
out a yowl and raced wildly about, kids scattering in all
directions. The cat streaked over the table, upsetting a vase
of flowers and celery set in a water tumbler, then bounded
to the window curtains and clawed up them, while the
boys whooped happily and the girls squealed in fright. My
father waited for the right moment, as the cat raced past
him, then plucked off the clothespin. The hymn continued.

Finally, there was the Christmas dinner: an enormous
turkey, with cranberry sauce, heaping mounds of dressing
and mashed potatoes; gravy, corn, salad, nuts, pickles, bread
and butter, three-layer white, yellow, and chocolate frosted
cakes; a half-dozen pies: mince, apple, peach, and pumpkin.

But first we had the blessing. From the head of the table my father surveyed his family, and that year bestowed the honor on one of the younger boys, Nellie's son Granite. We bowed heads, smelling the lovely bouquet of the banquet. And then the young supplicant implored fervently, "And, dear Father, protect us from the tomcats." The table exploded in laughter, after which my father said, "Amen."

It was later, near bedtime, that the final treat came each year. This was the latest installment of the never-ending adventures of Jack, Leonora, and Rain-in-the-Face, two enterprising white youngsters and their Indian pal. My father sat in the center, his wives and children spellbound by the latest episode. Master storyteller that he was, he always stopped with our beloved characters in a situation of peril, to be extricated in the next installment.

He was completely happy on those occasions, except for one thing. My mother had a hired girl who was ugly, surly, and not very bright. "Nettie, why on earth do you keep that scarecrow?" he asked. "Why don't you get a better girl?"

"Because, John," she said with a bright smile, "You might marry her."

The next morning after these times together, my father was gone, off on one of his many gigantic enterprises, and the wives returned to their individual homes. But because my father loved "occasions," we could look forward to another gathering of the clan on his return.

My father's fond dream was for the clan to be self sufficient; thus the two Provo fruit farms and our brick barn, which were intended for family industry. Aunt Nellie ran a millinery shop in town to keep the girls busy, while the boys manufactured the Two-Step Ladder in our barn.

The arrival of my father with this marvelous invention was perhaps the most memorable of Santa's second comings. The Two-Step Ladder had no rungs. There were metal plates for the feet, which slid up and down two slotted boards. The plates curved over the toes, and a gentle lift caused the plate to rise a step, then lock as the weight settled on the heel. The descent was likewise controlled with pressure by the toes. The Two-Step Ladder was a most marvelous device when everything worked, but a menace to life and limb, as I can personally attest, when everything didn't, which was often. However, we loyally believed the collapse of this manufacturing enterprise was due to a whispering campaign by the "Ladder Trust."

Looking back, I can only marvel at my father's complete enjoyment of his tremendous family, which would have driven a lesser man up the wall. His wives weren't of the submissive harem type. On the contrary, they were women of spirit and great dedication to an ideal, with the courage to embark on the demanding and often heartbreaking requirements of "the Principle," devoting their lives to a test designed to be a trial by fire to burn the dross from the gold.

I certainly can testify after knowing the wives and interviewing them as an adult, to the character of each one, which was refined in the furnace of adversity. The very Principle itself, unpopular within the Mormon culture, and practiced despite the harshest opposition of the U.S. government, was abandoned by The Church of Jesus Christ of Latter-day Saints during their lifetime. In fact, my father, an apostle in the Church, fell from grace rather than deny his later wives. He paid an enormous price for his family, but never expressed regret for the bargain.

It is little wonder that the offspring of such parents were individualists. My brother Cliff (Aunt Nellie's) was one of the more high-spirited of the clan. One time he and Paul Brimhall, son of the president of Brigham Young University, decided to chuck school and see the world. They boarded a freight train at Provo, crawling through the ice compartment of a refrigerated car. The train crew shut and locked the hatch, and the boys weren't discovered until the train stopped to re-ice at Pocatello, Idaho. My father received news of Cliff's whereabouts calmly, advising authorities to hold the boys until he sent someone for them, then submit a bill for board and room. Cliff and Paul cooled their heels for thirty-two days in jail before Paul's older brother arrived for them. Thoroughly cured of wanderlust, Cliff reported to my father's office in Salt Lake City expecting further punishment. Instead, he was outfitted top to toe with new school clothing, and as my father put Cliff on the train for Provo, he said, "Son, next time you decide to see the world, tell your mother and me, for we love you."

My father's premature death, when I was eight years old, put an end to Santa's multiple visits and left his huge family of youngsters in a precarious position. Juvenile delinquency is a major problem with fatherless families. Yet while I won't pretend that we were all angels, particularly in my own case, I consider it remarkable that not a single child became a police problem. The strength of my father's personality remained behind with us. Though he was gone, *he was there.* My mother always spoke of him in hushed tones. His precepts and maxims were our rules of conduct. The strongest reproof my mother had, when I got into mischief, was to ask what Father would think of such doings. *He was there.*

SCHOOL DAYS

Reed Smoot had become a U.S. Senator, but the "Y" wasn't a University yet when I began kindergarten at Brigham Young Academy in Provo, with Ida Smoot Dusenberry as my teacher. I wasn't too fond of kindergarten because, despite my angelic behavior, Ms. Dusenberry would frequently tie me up with a rope and chuck me into a black closet. While I never complained, the curriculum did seem monotonous. Later, when my mother asked what I'd learned, I would say truthfully, "To take little bites." During the course of the year this was all there had been time for, outside the closet.

Being of a modest nature, I never told my mother that I was receiving such special attention. I figured she had enough troubles of her own. She was baffled when I refused to continue my education at the BY Academy, but decided to enroll me in the first grade at Parker school. My teacher was Edith Young, a granddaughter of Brigham. Miss Young had no rope or closet, but she did have her class divided into the Robins and the Bluebirds. I found myself in the Bluebird ghetto until nearly Christmas, when Miss Young promoted me to the Robins upon discovering that I had memorized the first grade reader and was bringing Black Beauty to school to while away the time.

In the second grade, Miss Andelin consigned me again to the Bluebirds, until she found the reason for my inattention: after mastering the school texts, I'd been bringing Horatio Alger books to class and devouring one each week. Then in the third grade Miss Bean cast me to the Bluebirds once again, until the day I spelled the class down. She told me, at the end of the year, that if only one student in the class could be promoted, it would be me.

The next year, Jimmie Hickman not only consigned me to the Bluebirds but put me on Poverty Row. Poverty Row was a row of desks occupied by the extremely "dumb" kids. Hickman, however, was a mental case. He would hurl a book at a student who whispered. He ruled by terror. Things got so bad that the parents held a meeting attempting to have him discharged. He swore all claims against him were false. And he stayed on. After this, I realized that the twig was permanently bent, and I accepted the fact that life consisted of Robins and Bluebirds and that I could never expect to get along with authority. I haven't changed my mind.

Growing up in Provo, however, I never questioned the exhortations from the pulpit to remain unspotted from the wicked outside world; to be in, but not part of its iniquities and abominations. But though the spirit was willing, the flesh, alas, was weak. The day before I was to be baptized at age eight, I took advantage of the fact that my sins were to be washed away by going out behind the barn and swearing. I knew just four cusswords—hell, damn, bastard and son-of-a-bitch—but I put my heart into sinning while it didn't count.

Not long after my baptism, my father died and my schooling after that had to be scheduled around necessary work. Even young boys like me were needed to help keep things going. That first year after my father's death, I was put on a train to go help my brother Raymond out on my brother Joseph's ranch.

"Clinton!" the conductor called, coming into the compartment. He handed my straw suitcase down from the overhead rack. "This is your stop, boy."

As the train rounded a bend, the tiny town came into view, a half dozen houses, a store, a pole corral and a loading platform. Several inhabitants stood by the tracks enjoying the big event of the day—the arrival of the train.

My brother Raymond was waiting in a rig, wearing a big sheepskin coat on that nippy October day. I hopped off the train and ran to the rig, calling a greeting.

"Shut up!" Raymond snapped. "Climb in and let's go."

I climbed over the wheel and sat beside him. "What's the matter, anyhow?"

"Quit grinning like an ape," he growled. He drove along a dirt road that meandered among low hills grown with sage, cedar, and scrub oak. "For hell's sake act a little solemn, can't you? Dad died three weeks ago. People will wonder what the hell you're laughing at."

I didn't know what to say. My father had been an infrequent visitor. We had had so few times together that I remembered every one of them. While there was emptiness and heartache for my mother's grief, somehow his presence remained. To me it was as if he was just away on one of his gigantic business deals.

By the time we reached Joseph's ranch, Raymond was his usual cheerful self. Our older brother Joe had married, and with his wife, Jennie, expecting a baby he'd taken a job in

Provo for the winter. Raymond went out to take care of the ranch, and Paul and I were to spend alternate months with him. Raymond was twelve, I was eight, and Paul was five. The ranch was fifteen miles from Clinton, and our nearest neighbors, the Oberhansleys, were four miles away.

We pulled up at the ranch house: a one-room, tar-paper shack with an attic, sitting in a little hollow beside a spring. I jumped off and drank deeply at the spring, watching the water bugs playing on the sandy bottom, until a sudden pain knifed through my temple from the ice-cold water.

"What did Mother send?" Raymond asked, when I opened my suitcase inside the farmhouse.

"Clean clothes for you and a batch of cookies."

"Cookies? Why the hell didn't she send bread?"

"What's the matter with cookies?"

"They're sweet. I can't make anything except cake."

"Why not?"

"Damned if I know. Bread or rolls just don't pan out."

He bit off the corner of a cookie dubiously then tossed it back. "Let's get at the chores; and I've got to fix the stove pipe tonight."

I followed Raymond out to the barn. "How'd you like it here?" I asked.

"Swell. No school. Nothing to do except the chores and send a weekly report to Joe."

There were two cows in the barn, a heifer, and a team of bay work horses, all branded XIX on the right ribs. I forked hay into the manger while Raymond cleaned the stalls; then I helped him milk. He finished his cow then took over mine while I fed the pigs and chickens. I never could milk fast enough to make foam in the pail the way he could.

After straining the milk, we forked a jag of hay on the rack, hitched up the bay team, and went over the hill to the range livestock. There was a beautiful sorrel mare in the pole corral, with a half-grown colt.

"Want to ride on my horse?"

"How come it's yours?"

"I'm gonna ask Joe to give Fifi to me." Raymond got a hackamore from the slab shed, then led the sorrel to the corral fence so we could climb on with Raymond in front. He kicked his heels in her ribs and we went at a lope across the sage of the flat, the colt running behind. "She's no good to Joe, so maybe he'll let me have her."

"No good? How come?"

"Balks."

He circled back to the corral. "I could sure cure her if she was mine, I'll bet."

"Can't nobody cure a balky horse. No good for nothing but fish food."

After we took the rack back over the hill and put the team in the barn, Raymond had to fix the stove pipe before he cooked supper. He'd bought a shiny blue length of pipe from the Clinton store, which he put in place of a section which had rusted through. The joint between the new and old pipe was wobbly, so he took the .22 rifle from the corner and shot through the joint, riveting the two together.

A couple of days later a man drove up in an old Overland. It had been a touring car, but he had chopped off the rear seat and built a crude truck body. On the door he had hand lettered, "J. Phillips—Junk and General Hauling."

"Hi, kids," he boomed. Phillips was a big man with a paunch, chewing on a match stick. One gallus of his bib overalls was fastened with a nail. A white ring on the bib pocket outlined his dollar Ingersol watch, the watch fob being a rawhide string looped through the top buttonhole. "Seen your brother Joe in Provo, and Joe, he said you got a balky horse out here."

"Sure have," Raymond admitted.

"I got a cure for that."

We got in the Overland and he jammed the gas feed to the floor, then let out the clutch. The car jumped like a rabbit, almost stalling the engine, then it chugged along, jerking, picking up speed until it ran as smooth as it could, still making an awful clatter with the homemade truck body bouncing about as we went over the hill. When we got to the corral, the sorrel mare and her colt trotted up, sniffing for feed.

"Beautiful mare," Raymond said, "if she didn't balk."

"We'll fix that, boy," Phillips said, chewing on his match as he surveyed the sorrel. "Plump, good shape. Joe, he said to make a offer and you'd send it in with your report. Tell him I'll give him twelve dollars."

"Twelve dollars?" Raymond echoed, incredulous. "For that beautiful mare?"

"What's she good for, boy? Just eating her fool head off."

"But you said you could cure her."

"There's one sure cure for a balky horse, boy—fish food. Feed her to the trout. I'll haul her to the hatchery. Tell Joe twelve dollars."

Before starting back, Phillips got out a can of neat's-foot oil and squirted some on the clutch. "Gotta be careful, or she'll slip; then you have to put on Denver mud." The clutch worked pretty well as we went back over the hill.

"Fish food," Raymond growled, when the truck clattered away. "If Fifi's only worth twelve dollars, maybe Joe'll give her to me for keeping care of the ranch this winter."

He wrote to Joe, and we took the letter in to the Clinton post office. Three days later we had an answer.

"Regarding Fifi, let Mr. Phillips have her. But try and get fifteen dollars. It's better than nothing, and a balky horse is just no good. I only kept her because of the colt, which is big enough now to get along. Raymond, I wish I could let you have the mare, but things are tight right now. . . ."

"What the hell use would I have for a horse, anyhow?" Raymond growled. He tossed the letter into the stove, then ducked his head and turned away.

On Saturday we drove in to Thistle for supplies. Thistle was a small mining town, but it was a metropolis compared to Clinton. The road in was blocked by a long freight train crawling along with a load of coal. A half dozen men had climbed atop the train and were throwing coal off the gondolas. "There's been a miners' strike," Raymond said. "The railroad bulls, they don't bother nobody who's getting in a winter's supply of coal." He handed me the lines and leaped off the wagon. "You pick it up and load up the wagon while I heave it off."

As Raymond neared the train, a burly man atop a gondola hurled a hunk of coal at him. Raymond dodged.

"Keep away, kid!"

"We need coal for winter!"

"Ain't no job for kids! I'll heave off a load for you!"

So we got our winter's coal, and just in time, for it snowed next day.

Except for Mr. Phillips, our only visitor was Kurt

Oberhansley, who rode over to the ranch every day at noon and would lie on the back of his white horse watching through the window as we ate our scrambled eggs and cake. Kurt was about my age. His older brother, Henry, had boarded with us while going to BYU and was Joe's close friend. It might have been that Henry sent Kurt over to see how we were getting along; I never knew. We never said hello to Kurt or acknowledged his presence until Raymond again tried to make biscuits. While they were baking we teased ourselves with the anticipation of steaming hot biscuits dripping with butter. A trick we'd learned to make the butter come was to dump a double handful of snow into the churn. Unfortunately, we'd cleaned a chicken at the spot where I'd scooped the snow that day. Even with the feathers combed out with a fork, the butter tasted awful and the biscuits were gray, soggy, and bitter. So when Kurt arrived at noon I took him out a plate of hot biscuits dripping with butter. He gobbled them up, then lay on the back of his white horse to watch through the window as Raymond and I went back to our scrambled eggs and cake.

Joe had a supply of popular fiction at the cabin. We read *Freckles, Girl of the Limberlost, Pollyanna,* the Tarzan books, Horatio Alger, *Trail of the Lonesome Pine,* Harold Bell Wright, B. M. Bower's *Chip of the Flying U,* and Zane Grey's *The Rainbow Trail,* sharing the light of the oil lamp. We were at the table reading one night when from the corner of my eye I caught a movement. A mouse was at the half-opened door of the closet. It hesitated, whiskers wiggling, then came across the floor and began eating the cake crumbs near the table. I caught Raymond's eye and gestured.

"Why, that's Alfie," Raymond said. "How are you, Alfie?"

As Raymond spoke, the mouse froze momentarily, then raced for the closet. Raymond slammed the closet door shut. "I always catch Alfie by the tail."

"Oh, sure," I jeered.

Then we heard a tiny squeal, and sure enough, there was the tip of Alfie's tail wiggling frantically at the crack of the door.

"I do it all the time," Raymond said. "It's a game we play."

On the second Saturday morning we cleaned the cabin, washed all the dishes, swept and even dusted because our sister Lillian was coming out for the weekend. "She's real fussy," Raymond said, "the way girls are."

Raymond and I met the train at Clinton. When we brought Lillian to the cabin she took one look and said, "By damn, I should have brought my vaulting pole! What a mess!" Then she squealed when she saw Alfie in a fruit jar on the window sill. "My hell, you're even raising mice in this pigpen!"

"That's Alfie," Raymond said. "He's real cute."

"We caught him by the tail," I said, "One night—"

"Either Alfie goes," Lillian said, "or I do."

I let Alfie loose outside and we never saw him again.

For supper that night we had cream of tomato soup with Parker House rolls—light, fluffy rolls that weren't sweet. Nothing could have been more delicious.

"You've got to show me how," Raymond said. So Lillian demonstrated, while Raymond watched intently and I wrote down the ingredients and directions for mixing. Now we had the secret.

After Lillian was gone, Raymond set out to stir up a batch of Parker House rolls, while I checked off the directions of the recipe. Once again we found ourselves tantalized by anticipation, waiting on hot rolls and melted butter, knowing this time that we had the secret. They came out of the oven looking like gray golf balls, and every bit as hard. We found that by cracking them with a hammer and soaking them in milk, they were edible. Then Raymond went back to cake.

Not many days later, the old Overland came clattering up to the ranch again. J. Phillips climbed out wearing the same greasy overalls and chewing on the same match. "Hi boys!" he boomed. "Come to pick up that balky mare. Been waiting till the fish hatchery could use the meat."

Raymond swallowed. We'd been trying to work Fifi, but every time we hitched her up with one of the bays, the mare balked before the job was done. If you tried to use a whip, Fifi would lie down and stay down until the harness was removed.

"Why, ah, Joe, he don't think twelve dollars is much for a fine mare."

"What does he want to do, let her eat her fool head off without getting no work out of her?"

"Joe, he said he wouldn't sell Fifi for twelve dollars."

Phillips chewed awhile on his match stick. "Tell you what I'll do, boys. On account I'm here and all, I'll give you fourteen dollars. But not a cent more." He undid a button of his shirt and produced a sheaf of currency fastened to his grimy underwear by a safety pin. "Here you go, boys."

"I'll have to write Joe if he'll take fourteen."

"Maybe I'd better write him. I think you kids just want that mare for a pet, huh?" Phillips got in the Overland and clattered away. Raymond looked at me bleakly.

"We'll hitch Fifi to the hayrack. Maybe she only needs more work."

Snow had drifted on the shoulder of the hill, making it an adventure every day to see if we could get around the curve without the hayrack tipping over. That afternoon as we drove over the hill with Fifi hitched to one of the bays, the rack began sliding down sideways. Raymond yelled at the team and cut them with the whip. The bay tried to lunge ahead, but Fifi stopped dead.

"Git up ya balky fool!" Raymond cut again with the whip. At this, Fifi proceeded to lie down.

The hayrack meanwhile was slipping downhill over the drifted snow. The wheels on the low side dropped with a sudden lurch.

"Jump!" Raymond hollered. But I was already in the air. We climbed out of the bitter cold snowbank to find that the rack hadn't tipped over. The rear wheels had slid around on the hill, holding the load upright. I had snow down my neck, in my hair, up my sleeves and pant legs, and in my shoes. I waded up through the snowbank and kicked Fifi in the ribs. "Damn you, you balky fool!"

Raymond was unhooking the harness of the bay. As I stooped to release Fifi's tugs, he said, "Wait a minute, Sam. Don't unharness her. Leave her be."

"How come? We got to put the bay team on the rack and get the hay down to the corral."

"Sam, you go back down to the house and bring the lasso rope." Raymond kneeled in the snow beside the sorrel.

"I'm going to have a little talk with Fifi."

I didn't try arguing with Raymond because he could out talk anybody in the whole Taylor family. I hurried over the hill to the cabin. My toes and fingers were tingling, so I stayed a few minutes by the stove before taking the lasso up to the rack.

Raymond was still kneeling beside the balky mare when I got there. "Now, Fifi," he said, "you think you're smart, but you're really dumb as hell. By balking you get out of a little work, but you'll end up feeding the trout. The smart horse is a good worker. In return it gets the best feed, the best stall, the best care. You're just a silly fool, Fifi, you and your balking act."

Fifi regarded him with stony contempt.

"Okay, Raymond," I said, "I'm cold and anyhow Fifi, she don't know what the hell you're talking about."

"How do you know how much she understands? If she's smart enough to get out of work by balking then she's got the brains to save herself from the trout farm."

"Horses don't know nothing except maybe a half dozen words, like whoa, git up, back up, and their names."

"Don't be too sure," Raymond said. "Do you know that the pioneers used to administer to oxen that went down by the laying on of hands?"

"Maybe so, but we can't administer. We're only kids. We ain't got the priesthood yet."

"The point is that if the pioneers could administer to an ox then I can talk sense to Fifi. Okay?"

"Go ahead and talk. But cut it short. I'm cold."

So Raymond talked sweet reason to the mare lying in the snow, while Fifi regarded Raymond in sullen silence. She'd learned her one trick well. She wouldn't move a muscle until the harness was removed.

"Well okay, Fifi," Raymond finally said. "You've had your chance. Sam, give me that lasso."

He lashed her forelegs together, then her hind legs, and then bound her legs to the tongue of the hayrack.

"Now, just try to get up, you damn fool!"

We both climbed on the bay. The warmth of the horse felt good to my chilled seat and shanks. Instead of returning to the cabin Raymond rode down the hill to the corral. He got a halter from the slab shed and put it on Fifi's colt, then led the colt up the hill and tied it to a clump of scrub oak not far from where the mare lay but out of her sight. The colt whinnied, and Fifi answered. We went on to the balky horse at the hayrack.

"Change your mind yet?" Raymond asked. Fifi made no indication that she had; she wasn't even trying to get up.

"Okay, it's your own damned fault." He kicked his heel into the bay's ribs and we went over the hill at a lope.

"What about feed for the range cattle?" I asked.

"They'll have to wait until morning."

"You're going to leave Fifi there in the snow all night?"

"She'll be snug as a bug in a rug in that snowdrift; it's like an Eskimo igloo. Anyhow, it's warming up, and the wind's changed. We'll probably have more snow tonight."

With night the coyotes began howling. We could hear Fifi and her colt calling to each other over the hill.

"What if there's a cougar around?" I said, as Raymond and I shared the light of the oil lamp after supper. We were trying to read, but I couldn't concentrate on the printed words. "Their favorite dish is horse meat."

"Serve her right." Raymond declared, trying not to show his worry. "Better a cougar got her than the trouts."

"The cougar will go for the colt."

"It's a chance we've got to take."

I generally was a sound sleeper, but it seemed as if I lay awake all night, listening to the coyotes and the whinnies of the colt and mare.

Next morning there was a half-foot of new snow, and it was still coming down. We were up early and didn't bother with breakfast. We harnessed one of the bays and rode him up over the shoulder of the hill. Fifi was still lying there, lashed to the tongue of the hayrack.

"You go get the colt while I untie the lasso, Sam."

As I brought the colt into view, Raymond jerked the last knot of the rope free then let loose with wild whoops and began flogging Fifi with the end of the lasso.

"Get the hell up or it's fish food."

Fifi lurched stiffly, clambering to her feet. And that's the last time she ever balked. I'll never know if it was because of being tied up all night or whether it was because of what Raymond said to her. Raymond could talk a bird out of a tree.

After that winter, Joe sold the ranch and Raymond and I went back to Provo and school. I'm sure that Raymond would have made an excellent rancher when he grew up, if John W. Taylor's blood in his veins hadn't made him an even better salesman and promoter.

We brought Fifi to Provo, but it soon was apparent that city life in a plural family was no picnic for a saddle horse. With all our brothers and sisters lining up for rides, Raymond wished Fifi would learn to balk again. She was overworked and her ribs began showing. When Raymond talked of selling her, the howl from the swarm of siblings prevented it.

I don't know how things would have turned out, except that Aunt Nellie's boy, Cliff, borrowed Fifi one afternoon. She was hungry and thirsty, and when he brought her back to his mother's barn, Fifi ran through the door at a dead run, wiping Cliff off at the lintel. Cliff wasn't badly hurt, but the accident provided an excuse for Raymond to sell Fifi to a farmer on the Provo bench.

Raymond always treasured the memory of the winter at Joe's ranch. Many years later, during the uranium boom, he would name a group of claims the XIX, Joe's brand.

CHAPTER 4

"UNCLE JACK"

During the summers my brother Paul and I worked on farms around Provo. It was school vacation, but I'm sure we learned more than we would have in the classroom. We learned the value of a dollar and the price of integrity.

On the last day of beet thinning one summer, Mother packed us a lunch in a paper sack, then Paul and I pedaled out onto the bench on our bicycles to "Uncle Jack" Sloat's. Uncle Jack was no relation. He was just a big, gruff guy who liked to be called uncle.

After two weeks of crawling along the rows of beets on hands and knees, pulling out every seedling except one in each clump left by the blocking hoe, our wrists were sore and our knees raw. We were glad this was the last day of thinning, even though I could do six rows a day and Paul four. At ten cents a row that was good money.

The last day of a job is always the longest, but as we crawled along over the sharp clods, with the blazing sun overhead, we encouraged each other by planning what we'd do with the money. Paul would have a little over four-and-a-half dollars coming, while I would have almost seven; at the ages of six and nine that was real money to us. Then too, this was the last of the beets, and from now on our work would be more fun—picking berries, cherries, apricots, peaches, and apples—things you could eat as you worked. Later in the fall there'd be the beets to top. We'd been too small for that job in years past, but I figured maybe this fall I could say I was eleven or twelve and get the job.

Finally we finished the last row of the field and went down to the house for our pay. As we came into the farmyard, Uncle Jack Sloat came out the back door with a sack of candy in his hand. "Help yourself, boys!" he boomed. "You sure done good work, and I appreciate it! Go on, take some more! Put some in your pockets!"

The bag held candy kisses that stuck to our teeth as we chewed. "Good, huh?" Uncle Jack Sloat thundered. He always talked in a loud voice, and he laughed in great booming bellows. He was a big man with a wide smile and great shocks of curly hair. Everybody called him "Uncle Jack" because he fit the type.

"Well boys, the job's done. Good-bye," Uncle Jack said. We ducked our heads in embarrassment, and then his great laugh boomed. "Thought I'd forgot about the eagle screaming, didn't you? Well, I didn't. Got your wages all figured up. Sam, you've got $6.90 coming, and Paul, yours is $4.60. Is that right?"

We nodded, mumbling as we chewed.

"Well, I'm not going to give you that much," Uncle Jack said. "You know why?"

We shook our heads.

"Because I'm going to give you more!" Uncle Jack bellowed, laughing. "Paul, I'm going to make it four dollars and seventy-five cents; and Sam, you'll get seven and a quarter. How's that, boys?"

We mumbled thanks as we chomped on the kisses.

"I always pay on the first of the month, to keep my books straight," Uncle Jack said. "Let's see, this is the seventeenth; the first will be two weeks from next Friday. Now, don't forget!"

As we rode off along the dusty road, Paul said, "He sure is a good guy, isn't he?"

I spat out the candy.

"What's the matter?"

I took the kisses from my pocket and threw them into the weeds of the ditch bank beside the road. "I don't want any of his damned candy!"

Paul got off his bike and went back to look for the candy. "If you don't want it, why don't you give it to me instead of throwing it away?"

I got off my bike and went back to help him search. After all, he might as well have the candy. I knew it was all we were going to get for two weeks of work. I'd worked for these "Uncle Jack" types before. I knew all about paying on the first of the month to keep the books straight. Paul was younger; he hadn't found out yet. And I wasn't going to tell him, with all the plans he'd made for that $4.60.

Mother never asked about the money we earned. She figured it was our own, and we were expected to keep care of it. I was glad of this when we got home because I didn't want to tell her we'd been fleeced by a sharper.

On the first of the month Paul and I pedaled out to Uncle Jack's farm again. It was only about three miles, but it seemed like ten to me. The big man was happy to see us. "I knew you boys would be here today for your pay. You're the kind that keeps an appointment. Yes sir, the kind you

can depend on. And I got your money for you. I've got the
checks all made out. But I can't give them to you today,
because I just made a deposit in the bank and it's got to
clear. That'll take—let's see, this is Friday—why don't you
drop back around on Tuesday?"

We did drop around on Tuesday. Uncle Jack wasn't
home. We went out again the next Saturday.

"Boys, I must of just missed you Tuesday," Uncle Jack
explained. Why didn't you wait? I had your checks all made
out and ready, but now the money's gone and we've got to
wait until the first. Can you for sure be here on the first of
next month?"

As we pedaled toward home, Paul said, "Do you think
he's ever going to pay us?"

"Oh, sure," I said.

He looked across at me, and then big tears welled up in
his eyes and began rolling down his cheeks. I could never
lie to Paul; he knew me too well. A lump grew in my throat
as Paul cried silently. We'd spent many an evening looking
at the Sears & Roebuck catalogue. I wanted a three-lens
magnifying glass, and Paul wanted a fishing tackle box.
We'd planned to go halvers on a book called *The Boy
Mechanic, 1000 Things for Boys To Make*; and we'd also go
halvers on an aluminum pan for Mother, something she
needed. As the lump in my throat grew bigger I resolved
that when I grew up, I would go to Uncle Jack's and beat
him up.

On the first of the next month we were working in the
cherries, and Paul didn't have the heart to go back to Uncle
Jack's. He was more a realist than I was, although I'd had
more experience. After getting through picking cherries I

rode my bike out to Uncle Jack's that afternoon. After the
dog began barking and nobody appeared at the door, I
knew he wasn't home again. Well, I was here and I'd stay
here until he came home, I decided. I sat down under a
tree in the yard to wait.

Presently I got tired of sitting and started wandering
about, looking at the pigs, the chickens, the cows and
horses, the barn and outbuildings, thinking how easy it
would be to get even with Uncle Jack. Then I decided I'd
better go, because if anything *did* happen while Uncle Jack
was gone, I'd be blamed. While I hadn't seen anyone in the
vicinity, I knew somebody always saw you. Just as I picked
up my bicycle was about to leave, a boy came down the
lane. He was bigger than me, about twelve years old.

"What are you doing around here, kid?" he asked.

"Uncle Jack said to come out today and get the money
he owes me."

"You'll never get nothing out of that old deadbeat without your dad comes out with you."

"My dad died."

"Then you'll never get a red cent. Uncle Jack is the worst
deadbeat on the Provo Bench. He never pays for nothing.
If he borrows something, you never see it again. Know
what he does at the grocery store?"

"No," I admitted.

"Well, he goes in a store where they don't know him, and
he gives them that big smile and all that stuff, and he buys
groceries for a week, money on the counter." The boy
slapped one palm atop the other, demonstrating. "Same
thing next week, money on the counter. Meanwhile, he's
been dropping by for a sack of Bull Durham or a candy

bar, being friendly. By the third week, he's pals. Then he says he don't have the money right now, but it'll be here Monday. And he pays on Monday. But next week he pays only part. And pretty soon he's in so deep the storekeeper can't cut him off without losing everything. After that he *really* runs up a bill. Only the finest. Uncle Jack's a big eater; so's his wife. And the same thing with shoe stores and hardware. Everything. He's a deadbeat. How much does he owe you?"

"Six dollars and ninety cents. But he said he'd give me seven and a quarter."

"Why didn't he tell you he'd give you ten bucks? It wouldn't cost him no more. His piano, the furniture, the stove—he don't pay for nothing. He gives them a down payment and a hard luck story; that's what my dad says."

"Why don't they come and take it back?"

The boy indicated the farm equipment sitting about the yard. "Look at that junk! By the time Uncle Jack's had something awhile, nobody *wants* it back. They just hope he'll give them a little on account. And he never says he won't. Like you . . . he'll never tell you that you won't get the money. He'll just keep stalling you off, making promises."

"Do you live around here?" I asked.

He nodded toward the east. "Next door. My dad's got a fruit farm. What's your name?"

"Sam."

"Mine's Bill."

"Hi."

"Well, why don't you go home? He won't never give you anything."

"I'm already here; maybe I better wait until he gets back." I had a notion to denounce Uncle Jack, though of course I knew I couldn't talk like that to a grown man.

Bill looked at me calculatingly. "You could get even with the old deadbeat. Ever thought of that?"

I'd thought of it, guiltily. "No," I said.

"Come here."

I went with him into the granary where there were a half dozen sacks of feed. One of the sacks was white, with the word *Poison* in big red letters. "That's for mice," Bill said. "All we'd have to do is mix some with the chicken feed, or with the oats for the horses. That'd get even with the old deadbeat, wouldn't it?"

"I'd get put in jail."

"Who would know anything about it? What are you afraid of?"

"I better not."

We went outside. Bill pointed to the cows in the pasture. One of them was reaching her neck through the fence. Her tongue curved out and captured a sprig of lucerne from the adjoining hay field. "All we got to do is let down the gate and let the cows in the lucerne. When Uncle Jack comes home they'll be laying in the lucerne with their feet up in the air, bloated. You ever seen a bloated cow?"

I shook my head. "No."

"Got a match?"

"No."

"One match, and Uncle Jack's barn and all the hay in it would make a hell of a big bonfire, wouldn't it?"

"Maybe I'd better go home," I said uncomfortably. "My mom will be wondering where I am."

"Mama's boy," he taunted. "Do you smoke?"

"Sure. All the time."

"Come on." He ran toward an old shack that sat behind the main house and disappeared inside. When I followed, the place was dim after the brightness outside, and I couldn't see Bill. The shack had once been the main house of the farm, but now it was used as a workshop and storage space. Originally it had had two rooms, but the partition had been taken out. What had been the ceiling of one room was now a loft, with a ladder nailed to the wall leading to it. The loft was piled with junk.

"Bill?" I questioned.

A deep voice said, "What are you doing in here, kid?"

I jumped, startled. Bill laughed, and I saw him amid the junk in the loft with his mouth to one end of a long length of tin drainpipe.

"Bet you thought Uncle Jack was back," he said, his voice hollow through the pipe.

He came down the ladder and opened a drawer of an old buffet that held carpenter tools and a harness. He took out a box labeled *Snap Rings*, opened it, and took out a half-filled package of cigarettes. "His wife won't let him sin in the house," Bill said. "She's real churchy. Sort of went off the deep end when their kid, Johnnie, got killed. Me and him used to play together. He got drowned in the irrigation canal."

Bill offered me the pack of cigarettes. I took one, trying to act natural and casual about it. I'd never smoked anything except cedar bark, pulled from the fence posts and rubbed between the hands to soften it up. We lit up. The smoke burned my eyes and made tears come.

"Can you inhale?"

"No," I admitted.

"Watch me." Bill drew smoke into his lungs, then it came out in little puffs as he talked. "I come over here and smoke all the time." He blew the remainder of the smoke out through his nose. I tried blowing some out of my nose, but it hurt too bad and now the tears ran out of my eyes. "You're bawling!" he scoffed.

"Am not!"

Bill put the snap ring box back into the drawer and pushed it shut. "Ever get drunk?"

"Sure. All the time."

He got a screwdriver from the workbench and pried at a crack in the floor. A section of flooring came up and Bill pulled out a gallon jug of deep red liquid.

"Know what this is?"

"Sure. Whiskey."

"Whiskey!" he mocked. "That's all you know about it. It's wine. Bet you ain't never tasted wine in your whole life!"

That was true, but I couldn't admit it. "Sure I have, all the time."

Bill put the jug on the bench then tilted it, his mouth at the spout, crouching down as the jug tilted, until the red liquid ran into his mouth. He took a big swallow then tilted the jug upright again and breathed a slow breath.

I did it the same way, but I took just a little sip. Even so, it was like liquid fire down my throat, burning right down to my belly.

"Good, huh?"

Right then I couldn't speak. As soon as I could, I said, "Sure."

"When Uncle Jack's away I come over here to smoke and get drunk all the time," Bill said. "Me and Johnnie used to do it, when his old man went to town or something. Guess that's why Johnnie drowned in the canal that day. He was drunk."

Bill took another drink from the jug. "I never go in swimming when I'm drunk. Got that much sense anyway."

"Does your folks know you get drunk?"

"Dad would take the razor strap to me." Bill took another drink, then pointed to the jug. "Go on."

I tilted the jug on the bench, with my mouth to the neck, and took another small sip. This one didn't burn as badly. My belly felt warm and my head was light.

Bill was taking another drink when suddenly from the yard came the great booming voice of Uncle Jack hollering, "Whoa-ah!"

Bill jumped and almost let go of the jug. Wine squirted all over his face and shirt. Through the dirty window I could see Uncle Jack and his wife in the yard, getting out of their rig.

"He'll whip us until we can't walk if he catches us at his wine!" Bill said. He corked the jug and put it back under the floor.

"Do your chores, Jack, and then you come right back to the house!" his wife said shrilly.

"Yes, indeed, Dumpling!" Uncle Jack said heartily. He unhitched the team and took them to the barn. Then, just as we were ready to slip out, his wife appeared, having changed her town clothes for a housedress. As she went into the granary, Uncle Jack came out of the barn. With big strides he came directly toward the shack where we were cowering and peeking out the dirty window.

Bill scampered up the ladder to the loft. I was right at his heels. We hid amid the junk. Down below, the door came open, then banged shut. I heard a drawer scrape open, then came the whish of a match struck on a pants leg.

"Ah!" muttered Uncle Jack's deep voice, "dying for a smoke."

There came the hollow thump of a floorboard then the gurgle of the jug. "Ah!" said Uncle Jack.

"Jack!" came the shrill voice of his wife. "Got them horses took care of?"

"Fixing this snap ring, Dumpling!"

Her voice came from the chicken run.

"Chick! Chick-chick-chick!"

Beside me, crouching in the middle of the junk, Bill grinned. I tried to grin in return but my face was stiff. I was scared. I noticed Bill's eyes were glassy. From below came the gurgle of the jug. "Ah!" sighed Uncle Jack.

Presently his wife's voice shrilled. "Jack! The cows are still in the pasture! You better get at that milking!"

"Yes, Dumpling!"

"You're not fixing no harness in there! I know what you're doing!"

Uncle Jack's voice came in a deep chuckle. "You just know the half of it," he rumbled to himself.

"I don't know why you don't quit that filthy tobacco before it leads to other things!" her voice shrilled. "Next thing you know, you'll be tampering with liquor!"

"I wouldn't never do that, Dumpling!" Uncle Jack called, and the jug gurgled again.

"Then women!" shrilled Dumpling.

"Not with you around, my beauty!"

"Fauh!"

We heard her footsteps going to the house, and then the screen door slammed. Bill smiled foolishly at me, and from below came another gurgle of the jug.

We remained there, crouched in the midst of the junk of the loft, for several minutes, while Uncle Jack finished his cigarette. Then I heard the heel of his hand strike the cork of the jug and the hollow sound of the floorboard dropping into place. At just that instant Bill let out a sudden burp. We were crouched beside the length of drainpipe and Bill burped into the end of it. The sound was magnified into a hollow blurt.

From below came a couple of seconds of dead silence. Then: "What's that?" Uncle Jack's voice asked sharply.

Bill burped again.

"M-me," Bill said.

We were caught like the proverbial rats in a trap. The big man, half drunk, would give us a good whipping.

And then came the man's voice, different, awed.

"Johnnie . . ."

Bill turned to look at me, and there was a desperate something in his glazed eyes.

"Johnnie," came the voice from below, trembling with emotion. "Is that you, son?"

Bill gave a desperate shrug—there was nothing to lose—and put his mouth to the tin drain pipe.

"Daddy . . ."

"Oh, Johnnie, Johnnie, my boy . . ."

"I got drowned in the canal, Daddy, because I was drunk . . ." And as if to emphasize it, Bill burped again.

"Oh, Johnnie! Forgive me! Forgive your father's sins . . ."

Bill would have continued, but I put a hand over his mouth. He was tipsy and didn't realize what might happen if the big man discovered the ruse. From below came the sound of Uncle Jack blubbering with repentance. Then there was a crash as he rammed his heel through the floorboard, a shattering tinkle as he smashed the jug. He lurched out of the shack, blubbering, and we scooted down the ladder. When he disappeared inside the house, we slipped out of the shack. I carried my bicycle across the field, so as not to be seen going down the lane, and then rode for home.

Uncle Jack called that very night to pay Paul and me what he owed us. His face was shining with an inner light.

I still have the three-lens magnifying glass I got from Sears & Roebuck, and, so far as I know, Uncle Jack Sloat was a changed man to the day of his death. From the day of the miraculous experience of hearing his dead son's reproving voice, Uncle Jack reportedly never touched another drop of liquor nor smoked another cigarette. He attended church regularly and sang loudly. Of course the basic trouble with Uncle Jack was that he was a shiftless bum who was dedicated to getting through life as easily as possible, and that's a matter of character, not religion. So after his reformation, Uncle Jack didn't purposely beat anybody out of a bill anymore—he just was occasionally unable to pay.

CHAPTER 5

WHERE THE WEST BEGINS

One fall, the family went down to the Denver and Rio Grande station to see Rachel off as she left to teach school. When the train pulled out, Rae waved good-bye from the coach window, and Mother's eyes brimmed full with tears at the prospect of not seeing her eldest daughter until the next spring.

But the next day, Rae was home again. Seemed that the school board, after having given her a contract, selected another teacher without so much as notifying her. What about the contract? "Sue us," they said.

With no time to look around for a new job, Rae took the only one available at that late date, teaching the first four grades at a two-room school at Ibapah, a remote settlement on the Utah-Nevada line near the Goshute Indian reservation.

For vivacious and popular Rae, it was like being buried alive. Ibapah wasn't even a town, just two stores a mile apart in the Deep Creek Valley, the post office in the front room of the Chastain's log home, and a red brick schoolhouse sitting alone in the greasewood and sage.

Deep Creek, outlined by a string of willows, ran down the valley, with occasional ranches beaded along it. Rae's long letters were full of the unrelieved monotony of this hick place inhabited by cowboys and Indians. She could hardly wait to come home for Christmas vacation.

Before long, however, the letters dwindled to brief notes telling how nice the people were when you really got to know them, about the charm of the valley, and what a wonderful time she was having. She didn't really have time to get home for Christmas.

Mother knew what had happened. She wrote for Rae to come home for the holidays—and to bring her cowboy along.

Clarence Felt was tall, dark, and ruggedly handsome, with broad shoulders and a lean torso and hips. In fact, he matched the stereotype of the typical cowboy so well that it was almost impossible to find a suit to fit him. On the way to Provo, he and Rae spent a day shopping in Salt Lake before finding a suit (extra long, extra slim) that he wore for best some twenty years because he couldn't find another to fit.

Mother withheld her approval of the match for two reasons. One was that Clarence smoked hand-rolled cigarettes; the other—that he wasn't LDS. There was no church at Ibapah so his religious education was limited. The more he saw of Rae, however, the better Mormonism looked to him, and he converted. Mother then gave her blessing to the match, though Clarence still had the tobacco habit. They were married the next spring.

That fall I went out to live with Rae and Clarence on the Felt ranch for the school year because Mother was worried about my health and possibly, my disposition. The flu epidemic was still raging at the time, and I wore a gauze face mask on the train. Rae and Clarence met me at Wendover then drove the fifty miles across the desert to Ibapah. The valley was bounded on the west by flat-topped hills, while to the east across the sweep of sage and greasewood, were high mountains dominated by Old Baldy. The Felt store and ranch house were made of logs, sheathed inside and fitted with gasoline lights fed from a central pressure tank with hollow wires. Rae and Clarence had a two-room apartment above the store.

"Like oatmeal?" Clarence asked at breakfast.

"Sure."

He grinned. "You'd better."

"It's the dishes," Rae explained. They were using the set which were being given away with oatmeal sold at the store. Each package contained a coupon picturing the dish awarded for that purchase. The grand prize featured on the outside of the cartons, was a tureen pictured in full color, steaming with chicken and dumplings.

Even as Rae explained about the dishes, footsteps ascended the stairs. Clarence's father came in, tall and lean, with the stub of a cigar in his mouth. "I'll need a soup plate," he said, presenting a coupon. Rae gave him the dish from the cupboard.

The packages of oatmeal in the store were down to nine when Clarence suggested that he buy them all to protect their dishes.

"What?" Rae said. "We've had oatmeal for breakfast, oatmeal cookies, oatmeal muffins, fried oatmeal—I've got oatmeal coming out of my ears. Let them *have* the tureen."

"It's not just the tureen. There's the big platter, the teapot, and the salad bowl among those nine packages."

"How do we know?" Rae said. "Maybe somebody got the tureen coupon long ago or maybe a traveler or sheepherder got it. Indians rarely bring in coupons. Who knows?"

The red-white-and-blue stakes of the Lincoln Highway ran through the valley. Tourists in cars loaded with camping gear and with several spare tires lashed to the back stopped for gasoline or supplies (including oatmeal) at the store, then continued on their way.

"We can't afford to take the chance," Clarence said.

"Oh, all right," Rae said. As Clarence went downstairs to make the purchase, she mused, "What'll I do with it? Maybe make a big batch of cookies for the next dance."

I'd had enough oatmeal that I can't eat mush to this day. "Why not use it on the schoolhouse floor to make it slick for the dance?" I suggested.

"Instead of cornmeal?—that's an idea!"

Clarence came upstairs with seven packages of oatmeal balanced in his arms. "Couple of Indians got two packages ahead of me, Yellowhair and Jim. Hope they didn't get the tureen. I know how much you want it."

"What would Indians want with a tureen?" Rae said.

"They'd *never* bring that coupon in," Clarence agreed.

That night we had chicken and dumplings for supper, served in the tureen just like on the oatmeal box. Perhaps because I was trying to be extra careful as I dried the dishes, I dropped the tureen. It struck the floor, bounced, and lit right side up, unharmed. Then as I happily picked it up, it struck the iron frame of the cot I slept on and shattered.

"Well, that's one worry off my mind," Rae said. "I've been in suspense about whether we'd be able to keep that tureen ever since Clarence and I got married."

The very next day Yellowhair came down from the reservation with the coupon for the tureen. Yellowhair was a tribal leader and spokesman for the Indians when they hired out for sheep shearing or other work.

"Take down the teapot, salad bowl, and platter," Rae said to Clarence. "Give him his choice."

I followed Clarence downstairs to the store. Yellowhair was tall and muscular, wearing a beaded belt and hat band. He was sporting a pair of new shoes, worn just as he'd purchased them, with the laces knotted through one eyelet and left dangling, along with the price tag and the little booklet extolling their virtues.

"The tureen got broke," Clarence said. "So you can take your choice of these nice pieces."

Yellowhair poked a determined finger at the picture of the tureen on his coupon. "Him."

"No got. Shattered. Busted. Here, take any two of these."

"Him."

Clarence sighed. "Okay, we'll order a tureen for you. Come back next month. Okay?"

"Okay."

When the salesman for the wholesale house came through, he said, "Sorry, but we're all through with that china deal. Don't have a dish left in stock."

Clarence and Rae got out the Sears & Roebuck catalogue that evening. There was a set of open stock dishes with a somewhat similar pattern of red roses. They ordered the tureen, which came a couple of weeks later.

"Beautiful," Rae said. "Thank goodness that's off our minds."

"I was getting a little worried," Clarence admitted. "Shearing's coming up, and we might have a hard time hiring Indians if Yellowhair's nose was out of joint."

Yellowhair arrived at the store three days later and presented the coupon. "Him."

"You bet!" Clarence got the tureen down from a high shelf out of harm's way. "Here you go!"

Yellowhair looked from the tureen to the picture. He poked emphatically at the coupon. "Him!"

Rae came in as Clarence tried to pacify him. "It's not exactly the same pattern," Clarence said, "but this is the best we can do. Take it anyhow and we'll give you a couple boxes of oatmeal to boot."

Yellowhair exhibited the coupon. "Him!"

"Okay, we'll try again. Meanwhile, we start shearing next week. You bring Indians, huh?" He opened and closed his fingers twice, indicating twenty workmen.

"No shear. First, *him!*"

"Just a minute," Rae said. "Yellowhair, let me see that coupon." She examined it, then suddenly she beamed. "You wait a few minutes," she said. "Clarence, give them some soda pop. I won't be long."

Clarence uncapped three bottles of strawberry pop, one for Yellowhair, two more for me to take out to the wife and child in the buckboard at the hitching rack. The Indian family soberly sipped the pop, kept at room temperature for their benefit. It was a special treat, and they made it last.

They'd finished the pop and were waiting in the store when Rae called, "Hold the door open, Sam!" She came downstairs and into the store with the tureen. She put it on the counter in front of Yellowhair, then lifted the cover.

"Him!" she declared.

The tureen was now filled with chicken and dumplings, just like the picture on the coupon. Those who think the impassive redskin can't smile should have seen the double row of gleaming teeth.

"Him!" Yellowhair cried happily.

He and his family sat in the shade of the buckboard while eating the contents of the tureen.

"Lucky I was planning that for supper," Rae said. "The chicken was just about done, but I sure made those dumplings in a hurry."

When the last morsel was eaten, Yellowhair cast the tureen like an empty tin can into a clump of greasewood, then headed for the reservation in the buckboard. I rescued the tureen, which Rae happily washed and put away.

In the spring I helped Rae put in a vegetable garden. Clarence had plowed an area, though without much enthusiasm. "Never had much luck with vegetables out here," he said.

"What do you *do* for fresh garden things?" Rae asked.

"Do without."

Rae set her lips and mailed off an order for seeds. When they arrived I helped with the planting.

The seeds popped up on schedule, and Rae was out cultivating every day.

"What a wonderful place for a garden," Rae said. "There are hardly any weeds."

"Weeds won't grow here," Clarence said.

Rae gave him a strange look. "You just don't like to garden."

"I admit that."

"We always had a big garden at home. Mother's vacant lot fed our boarders all summer, everything but meat."

Presently, the ground of the garden began to harden. We irrigated it, but this just seemed to make the earth settle firmer, and two weeks later a hoe rang on the concrete-like surface with a metallic clang.

"What on earth is wrong with this soil?" Rae asked.

"Told you we never had much luck with gardens."

"I think the radishes might be ready, but I'm blessed if I can dig them out of the ground."

Clarence got a pick and went out to the vegetable garden. It was like digging into rock, but after ten minutes he'd chipped up a dozen or so radishes. Rae washed them and put them on the table. After the fight for survival in this hostile environment, they were little more than stringy roots with a flavor like horseradish. I ate half of one, with plenty of bread and butter; my eyes were streaming with tears and my tongue was on fire.

"I'm so hungry for green things I could die," Rae said, "but these are awful."

"Herman the hermit always has a good vegetable garden," Clarence said.

Rae's face lit up. "Would he sell us a few radishes?"

"Nope. But he'd give us some if we went out there and ate out of the garden. He won't sell anything, though."

"Well, why don't we go? Do you know him well enough?"

"Sure. But I don't know whether it's worth it."

"Of course it's worth it!" Rae cried. "I'm almost ready to go home for a visit, just to get something to eat besides bread, meat, and potatoes!"

"Well, all right," Clarence said. "But, remember, Herman's a hermit."

"Does he hate people?"

"Nope," Clarence said. "That's the trouble—he really likes people."

"Clarence," Rae said, "there are times when I don't appreciate your rustic sense of humor." Then she said to me, "Sam, why don't you ask Mr. and Mrs. Felt if they'd like to go along?"

I went over to the main ranch house. Mrs. Felt was in the kitchen. "Out to the hermit's?" Clarence's mother said. "Tell Rae thanks a lot, but I'm baking bread."

There wasn't much of a road the last couple of miles to Herman's, so we went in a buckboard instead of driving the Model T roadster or the Pathfinder touring car. Herman lived in a canyon that was steep, narrow, and choked with oak brush and boulders. It hardly seemed habitable until we broke into a little hollow where we came upon his log cabin and beside it, the vegetable garden.

"Just *look* at those vegetables!" Rae cried. In the mountain loam carrots, radishes, onions, turnips, and beets thrived. A row of peas stood waist high on their stakes.

Herman wasn't home. On the door of his cabin hung a little sign: "At mine. Back in an hour." Other signs sat in a box beside the door. "To Spring. Back in 10 min." "To Privy. Back immediately." "To Store. Back in two hours." "Milking. Back in 15 min."

"Poor fellow," Rae said. "He's just dying for company."

"I wonder what would happen," Clarence said, "if we just took a few radishes and left a note for him?"

"That would be mean," Rae said. "He's got all those signs

already made, just so nobody will leave without saying hello."

"Well," Clarence said, "you've had your chance."

Before Rae could ask him what he was hinting about, Herman hurried into view. "Seen you from up at the mine," he said, "and I sure didn't want to miss you folks."

As Herman continued talking, Rae looked at Clarence awkwardly, for Clarence hadn't introduced her. But Clarence was looking absently toward the vegetable garden, so she said, "I'm Rae Felt."

To say it, she had to speak quickly when Herman paused at a comma in his monologue. Herman paid no attention to what she said, but, with a reproachful glance at the interruption, kept on. He told us about his mine, he told us about his garden. He told us how he made his own deerskin clothing, how he cut his own hair. He was full of stories, one blending into another, with never a pause between.

The sun went down and with the twilight, Rae tried several times to ask Herman if we might have some vegetables. But the steady stream of his monologue would rise and fall effortlessly, overwhelming her voice with a torrent of words.

Rae looked bleakly at Clarence, who gave a little jerk of his head toward the garden and started that way.

"Sam, you bring the bread and butter from the buckboard," Rae whispered to me, while Herman glared at her inattention. Then she followed Clarence to the garden, and Herman went along, pouring out the words.

We pulled radishes and onions, eating them with the bread and butter we'd brought along. It was impossible to ask Herman if this was okay, to thank him, or to comment on how good things tasted. Herman's voice was like a mechanical thing: ceaseless, tireless, and oblivious to those he was supposedly addressing.

We finished the supper, and it got dark. Herman ushered us into his cabin, telling how he built it, how he barked the logs, and how he made the furniture. One word followed another endlessly, and I became acutely conscious of needing to relieve my bladder. A number of times I tried to ask where the place was, but Herman's barrage smothered me. When things reached a point of crisis I just dashed outside.

It was lovely under the desert moon, with the mountains looming up all around, the cabin with the yellow light at the window, the horses standing at the buckboard. I hated to go back into the cabin.

When I went inside, Rae and Clarence sat with glazed eyes, while Herman was now getting his second wind. His voice became stronger as he told in infinitesimal detail how to carry a backpack. He got down on the floor, pantomiming, showing how to get the arms into the straps. Then he began getting up, but fell backwards under the imaginary load, recovered himself, struggled erect and—within ten long minutes and endless thousands of words—we knew how to carry a backpack, if the information might someday come in handy. Without pause the story had blended into bear grease (which was, Herman said, good for the gut) and how to catch a bear.

There was a tin alarm clock atop the bushel box that was nailed on the wall for a cupboard. It got to be nine o'clock and Herman was showing no sign of fatigue. It got to be ten o'clock. Several times Rae tried to break in with "Thank you very much, but—" and "Well, it's getting late—" and

"My, I didn't realize we'd stayed so long." But Herman squelched such polite attempts at competition with no effort and kept on.

I got sleepy. Rae was trying to smother yawns. Clarence had run out of tobacco and was getting wormy, picking around among the stubs of his hand-rolled cigarettes looking for something worth relighting.

It got to be eleven o'clock and Herman's voice was like iron, his delivery vibrant. It got to be midnight and my head kept falling forward into the stream of his words. It got to be half past twelve. It got to be quarter to one in the morning.

Rae looked at Clarence. Clarence nodded. They arose and started out. Herman raised the speed of his delivery a notch, giving them no chance to get a word in edgewise, let alone "good-bye," which is almost two words. We simply walked out in the middle of a story. Herman followed us to the buckboard, talking. Clarence hitched the team to the rig and we climbed in. Herman followed down the canyon, telling a story as we drove away. Clarence snapped the lines on the rumps of the team and Herman couldn't keep up. His voice faded in the distance as he fell behind.

Nobody said anything until we were out of the canyon and headed across the sweep of the valley floor toward the ranch.

"No *wonder* he's a hermit!" Rae said. "He *couldn't* live around people!"

"That's right," Clarence said. "The hermits I've met aren't people who want to get away from it all. They're driven away."

I didn't remember reaching the ranch. I'd fallen asleep

and Clarence carried me in to bed. Next morning it was all like a bad dream, including the lingering taste of onions.

A few weeks later visitors came to the ranch, the sister of Mrs. Felt and her two daughters. We all had dinner in the main ranch house, and Mrs. Felt's sister asked, "What do you do for vegetables out here?"

"We just do without," Rae said firmly.

WE ALWAYS CALLED THEM GUESTS

When Mother lost the Donovan mansion in the final family financial crisis before Father's death, she scraped up enough from the sale of some sheep she'd inherited, plus a few hundred dollars she had squirreled away from her previous boarding business, to make a down payment on another house. She chose a decrepit eyesore of former red-brick elegance that had been built by George H. Brimhall when he was president of Brigham Young University. Mother was determined to transform the old building into a proper boarding house which would give her a dependable income. The family launched a remodeling project which involved electric wiring, plumbing, new floors and roof, screens, wallpaper, paint, and four sturdy porches to brace the old rock foundation at all sides. In addition, we fixed up a cottage at the rear into a rental unit, built a sleeping annex, excavated a basement, built a chicken coop, a storehouse, and a coal shed. I was five when this project began; I grew up with it.

We were the original do-it-ourselves kids. None of my sisters could remember *learning* to sew, cook, and keep house, nor could my brothers recall a time when they learned to use a square, saw, level, plane, and hammer—

but we all could do these things just the same because Mother put us all to work the minute we were able. Her delicious cooking attracted boarders to fill every room that we finished. With our large house full of roomers, and nearly two dozen boarders at the table three times a day, the girls were helping in the kitchen almost as soon as they were out of diapers. The boys kept busy at the perpetual building program, which in my case occupied some twenty years.

Our home in Provo adjoined the Fourth Ward meeting-house, and I think I enjoyed the Sunday morning services more than anyone else in the ward, for I could listen to them without getting out of bed. Week after week I was awakened by the lively opening song:

> Never be late for your Sunday school class,
> Come with your bright shining faces;
> Cheering your teachers and pleasing your God—
> Always be found in your places.

As a family we didn't see too much of the inside of the meetinghouse. We all had jobs or were needed to help Mother. I got my first steady work at eleven and at four-teen, trying to look older, began at the Knight Woolen Mills. Five of us, in turn, worked at the woolen mills, and all of us went to Brigham Young University, just two-and-a-half blocks from home, as soon as we were old enough. We kept time by the university bell, which tolled twice every hour.

With twenty or more boarders to feed three times a day, Mother didn't have time for church-going or much other outside activity. She arose at five, after baking nine loaves of bread every night before going to bed at midnight. She was haunted by the fear of oversleeping and not having meals on time. She set her alarm clock fast and put it on a chair by her bed, together with a teacup and a box of kitchen matches. Each morning the cup was full of burned matches—from checking the time in the night and making sure the clock hadn't stopped. When I rigged an electric extension for her, she wouldn't use it. The current might fail, she said, and she'd oversleep. The only outside activity I ever remember her having was always going to see "*The Birth of a Nation*," each time it came around. This film was enormously popular. She never missed a Harold Lloyd comedy either.

Although she wasn't a churchgoer, she maintained a quiet faith and passed it on to her children. Once a year she figured up her increase and paid the bishop one-tenth of it as tithing.

While our house happened to be physically near the chapel, in a sense everyone in Utah lives next door to the church. It is there, right "next door," part of daily life, whether or not you attend, whether or not you belong. As such, some of the Church's teachings became a part of Utah culture, as familiar to nonmembers as to the Saints themselves. One such doctrine was the Word of Wisdom, with its staunch prohibitions of "hot drinks," alcohol, and tobacco.

It is a bit difficult to explain to gentiles beyond the Zion Curtain about the Mormon attitude that developed toward coffee. Once a poll of students at Brigham Young University listed the use of this poison as the greatest of all sins, worse than adultery, worse than treason, and even worse than murder. There was something symbolic about it. To many, pouring a cup of the vile brew was more sinful than pouring hot lead into a baby's ear, although they could never explain why.

Some of the boarders in our boarding house were gentiles in the clutches of the coffee habit. Mother served them the poison because this was a business and she wouldn't inflict her religious views upon the paying customers. We kids were tantalized by the lovely aroma of the forbidden brew while we drank our Mormon tea—hot water, milk, and sugar. Tea and coffee were properly used only as medicines, and whether or not the therapy was party psychological, I know in my own case the value of such delicious dosages couldn't be denied.

One time during our boarding house years, my sister Lillian was being courted by a zealous young man who called for her at a time when preparations for supper filled the house with the scent of brewing coffee. After a horrified sniff, he decided to wait outside in the "pure air" while she got ready. He didn't say anything about the coffee that night, but the experience caused him to wrestle mightily with his soul for several days of torment. Finally, he made an appointment and arrived to talk things out.

"Lillian," he said solemnly, "I want you to be frank. There is something I must know. When I called for you the other day, I thought I smelled . . ." His voice trailed away, then he steeled himself and demanded, "Was it the smell of *coffee*?"

Lillian looked at him curiously. Since Mother ran a boarding house catering to gentiles as well as Mormons, the aroma of coffee at mealtime certainly might be expected. And why was he making it *his* business?

"Yes, you did," Lillian said rather sharply.

"Was anyone in the house sick?"

"No."

"Then the coffee was to be used as a beverage?"

"Yes."

"Well, then, considering how I feel about you, there is but one thing to do." The young man drew a deep breath. "Either your family must rise to my level," he declared, "or I must descend to yours."

To his amazement, Lillian received this solemn ultimatum with a wild shriek of laughter. The young man couldn't understand why he was unable to get another date.

Perhaps the most vigorous champion of the Word of Wisdom among our guests was Brother Jacobs, a middle-aged schoolteacher from Arizona who had come to get his Utah teaching credential at BYU. Brother Jacobs enjoyed going to the Lord's university. He wanted to teach at Salt Lake close to Church headquarters, and considered himself fortunate to be staying at a boardinghouse right next door to the Lord's meetinghouse.

Brother Jacobs was a big man, in fact a huge man, with a wide smile. But he just never quit pushing the Word of Wisdom at the table. When the coffee appeared, he would always remark about the poison in a smiling way. This nettled some of the gentile guests, and finally Mr. Smith, dean of our dinner table, took him to task.

"Now, look here, Jacobs," Mr. Smith said, "we don't bother you about our religious beliefs, and we'd appreciate it if you laid off about the coffee. A cup of coffee has absolutely no religious significance to some of us at this table."

"I'm not talking religion, I'm worried about your health," Brother Jacobs said.

"Let me worry about that, too," Mr. Smith said. "I don't want to live forever."

"Neither do I," Brother Jacobs said. "But I do expect to live to be five hundred years old."

Jaws dropped at the table as the guests gaped.

Brother Jacobs was *not* joking.

"How will you live to be five hundred?" Mr. Smith asked curiously.

"By living the Lord's law of health, that's how. In the Doctrine & Covenants, 89th section, we are promised health in our naval and marrow in our bones, if we eat according to the Word of Wisdom. We are told that the Angel of Death will pass us by."

"Oh," Mr. Smith said, "a religious belief."

"A *health* belief," Brother Jacobs insisted. "Section 89 means exactly what it says. If you obey the Lord's law of health the Angel of Death will pass you by. Pass the potatoes, please."

For his third helping, Brother Jacobs took a pile of potatoes big enough for two ordinary men, covering it with a half-pint of rich pork gravy. He heavily buttered a thick slice of homemade bread as he talked.

"I'm not a fanatic on the subject," he said, "but if the Lord makes a promise, he's bound by it. If I don't touch liquor or use tobacco, if I never drink coffee or tea, it will be up to the Lord to keep *his* end of the bargain." Brother Jacobs poured himself another glass of rich Jersey milk and tossed it down with satisfaction. "In the old days, men lived to be several hundred years old. It wasn't unusual at all. Look at Methuselah. He lived 969 years. All kinds of people got to be 500 or so in those days. And you know why? Because in those days they lived the Word of Wisdom. Then it was lost to the earth, until it was restored by the Prophet Joseph Smith."

"I see," Mr. Smith said. "How old are you now, Jacobs?"

"Forty-seven," Brother Jacobs said, "and sound in every bone, muscle, nerve, and fiber."

"And when will you retire from teaching, Jacobs?"

"When I'm seventy. There's a rule about that."

"Then what are you going to do for the remaining four hundred and thirty years of your life?" Mr. Smith asked.

Brother Jacobs grinned his wide grin. "I'll have a pension from Arizona and one from Utah. I'll take it easy." He reached for another thick slice of homemade bread. "If nobody's going to finish off that gravy, I'll just put it over this hunk of bread to keep it from going to waste."

A few weeks later, Brother Jacobs was felled by a heart attack and rushed to the hospital. Uncle Fred was his doctor and dropped in to say hello to Mother while making a call nearby.

"How is Brother Jacobs coming along, Fred?"

"Well, Nettie," Uncle Fred said in his slow and deliberate manner of talking, "physically he is doing as well as can be expected. These things take time. He's been digging his grave with his teeth. But if he takes care of himself from now on, there is no good reason why he won't live to be seventy."

"Seventy?" Mother exclaimed. "Good heavens—he expected to live to be five hundred!" She told Uncle Fred of Brother Jacob's faith in Section 89.

"That explains it," Uncle Fred said. "He's been very depressed, but I didn't understand why. This heart attack must be a severe blow to his faith as well as to his body."

"Perhaps now," Mother said, "he'll be humble enough to realize that the Lord's law of health *really* means moderation."

Perhaps he did, but we never knew, for as soon as he was able to travel Brother Jacobs went back to Arizona.

Most of our guests were not middle-aged, like Jacobs, but were young undergraduates at BYU, Mormons from small towns. The boys arrived off the farm with hay-balers' appetites, which made the line between profit and loss, at twenty-two dollars a month for room and board, rather thin for Mother. But the champion eaters of all time were the Presley brothers. They made a tremendous pair, hulking men who were the absolute epitome of the bottomless pit. Lillian, serving at their first meal, saw them divide the entire platter of meat between them, all the potatoes, all the corn. This created a crisis in the kitchen as Mother improvised for the other eighteen at the table. Lillian felt the meal was a nightmare as she watched in horrified fascination while the two Presley brothers ate food designed for twenty people. Finally it came to a thankful close as she served the apple pie. And then, bug-eyed, she watched the Presley brothers divide the ten thick slices of homemade bread remaining on the table, butter them lavishly, and eat them with a whole pie.

Lillian rushed into the kitchen and burst into tears. "Mother, they're eating us into the poorhouse!"

Mother, who had seen this sort of thing before, calmed Lillian and quietly went about preparing for the next meal. A week later the Presley brothers took to their beds, as she knew they would, and when they got well their appetites had adjusted to the sedentary lives of students—just in time to save her from financial ruin.

Another of our mother's boarding house guests was Mr. Miller, a businessman in town. We all liked Mr. Miller, and it was too bad he had to leave. But go he must, because Mr. Miller had, like a succession of others, fallen in love with Mother's cooking and had transferred his affections to the cook. Whenever a gentleman guest began patting us kids on the head in a fatherly manner, became fulsome in his praise of the food, and was seen eyeing up the property appraisingly, we knew that he was not long for our table.

Mother had no time for romance. In the boarding business her day began at five and ended at midnight. She was no doubt flattered when a male guest began finding excuses to drop by the kitchen for a chat, for a woman likes to know that she is attractive. But she simply didn't have the time to spare, even if she had had the inclination for romance, which she didn't. She felt that she had been honored to have married one of the choice spirits of her generation, and she couldn't think of uniting with a lesser man after John had gone. And so when an admirer got bothered enough to become bothersome, he soon was presented with some perfectly valid reason as to why his presence at the table would henceforth be impossible.

Some, like Brother Schneider, a German convert, kept emotions in check until they suddenly boiled over, whereupon they declared their undying love and wish to make Mother theirs. She regarded Brother Schneider's proposal practically. "It would be marriage only for this life. I am married to Brother Taylor for eternity."

This life, Brother Schneider said, would be fine; he would be content with half a loaf.

"There are the children," she said. Brother Schneider had five of his own under the care of a sister in Germany whom he was going to send for as soon as he had a place for them here. "That," she said, "would make a total of thirteen."

"But this is a big *haus*," Brother Schneider said. "Plenty off room."

"Yes, I suppose, with the guests gone."

Brother Schneider looked bleak. "No roomers? No boarders?"

"I certainly couldn't take care of thirteen children, a husband, *and* the guests," Mother pointed out, "even if we had the room, which we wouldn't have."

Brother Schneider, who earned a rather meager wage as a weaver at the woolen mills, gulped.

"And if I married again, I wouldn't want any more family," Mother said.

"At our age, babies? No, indeed, Sister Taylor."

"When I was carrying Paul, Brother Taylor and I decided that we had enough family. So from that time on we lived as brother and sister."

"Oh," Brother Schneider said bleakly.

He left at the end of the month.

Mr. Greene was a gentile, but as his admiration for the food and the cook increased, he became interested in Mormon doctrine. Once he began reading the Book of Mormon, he threw away his thick-lensed glasses; didn't need them any more, he said. Next he threw away his pipe. Then he got baptized.

Like many converts, he was red hot. Mother was happy to see him embrace the gospel, but wouldn't allow him to embrace her. The last straw came when he took up the cause of the Word of Wisdom with her, trying to get her to quit serving coffee to the gentile guests. When he lost the battle, he left at the end of the month.

We felt that our loss was the Lord's gain, until a few weeks later when we heard that his bicycle had collided with a car which he hadn't been able to see coming. The next time I saw him, after he got out of the hospital, he was pedaling along wearing his thick-lensed glasses and smoking his pipe.

Our star boarder was Mr. Smith, who was at our place year after year. Mr. Smith was a machinist for the railroad, with a quiet dignity which made him dean of the dinner table. When my brother married and left the table, Mr. Smith became, in a sense, head of the house though his domain ended at the dining room.

Mr. Smith kept his work clothing in his locker at the shops, so we never saw him in anything but a blue serge suit. He minded his own business, we minded ours. He had his religion, we had ours. And he also had the type of do-it-yourself reliance that we prized. When he got dental plates, they chafed him. After going to the dentist a couple of times, he undertook the job himself and spent three days working on the dentures at the shops. I have retained a mental picture of the giant equipment used for railroad maintenance employed for the precision work of shaping a set of dentures. How he did it I don't know, but the plates fit perfectly from that time on.

Mr. Smith had one idiosyncrasy, unusual for a man who

spent his working days in the bang and clatter of the railroad shops. At a sudden noise he would emit a sharp cry as if stabbed. Of course we respected Mr. Smith too much to tease him—yet, on the other hand, it was just too great a temptation for kids to bear. I remember my high point, when I came into the dining room with a bucket of coal while Mr. Smith was making a remark about the weather. "Yes, it's thawing—ach!" (as I dropped the skuttle to the floor)—"a little, but the paper says—ach!" (as I clanged the stove with the poker)—"that another storm—ach!" (as I banged down the draft)—"is coming." I never surpassed that, getting three outcries in one sentence.

Mr. Smith had two daughters, Mary and Helen, who went to school in Salt Lake and stayed with us in the summertime. Helen was a little younger than me and the most beautiful girl in the world. I took her on long rides on my bicycle, pedaling mile after mile, unmindful of trembling legs and bursting lungs, so long as she sat on the bar with her honey–blonde hair close to my face and with my arms around her as I steered the bike. She was my first love, pure and sweet and untainted by carnality.

None of the kids would have objected if Mother had married Mr. Smith, for we all liked and respected him. And, so far as I know, he was the only one who proposed who wasn't asked to leave. Mr. Smith was gentleman enough not to make it necessary; and again, perhaps Mother was attracted to him more than she admitted, even to herself. At any rate, it was good to have a head of the house, once my older brother Joe had married. It became even more important after Joe died suddenly at twenty-five.

Some two years after Father passed on, Mother had a dream. She dreamed that she walked through crowds of people, but was all alone. She walked along crowded streets, through buildings filled with people, into homes occupied by families and friends, but she was utterly alone. Somehow she awoke knowing that Joseph, her firstborn, was to be taken away from her.

Joe was home by this time, working in Provo and living with his wife and baby in the small rental unit behind the main house which we called the annex. He had given up the ranch at Clinton and had a job with the Taylor Brothers store (no relation). For Christmas that year he showered Mother with gifts, the most impressive being a Hoosier kitchen cabinet with a zinc worktable. She was subdued that Christmas, though we didn't know why. She hadn't told the family yet about the dream. She felt that Joe was obeying some impulse to do as much for her as possible while there was time.

The flu epidemic was on, but it hadn't hit our house. Transmission of the disease was believed to be spread by breath, and a local ordinance required everyone in Provo to wear a mask over the mouth and nose at all times in public. My mask, like that of most kids, was always moist, sticky, and filthy.

When the flu hit us, it hit hard. Everybody in the house was down, family and roomers—except Mother, Joe, and Paul. Mother brought in a nurse to help, and soon the mother of three brothers who roomed with us while going to BYU arrived to help out also. Joe's wife and baby were down with the malady as well. Joe cared for them and kept up the outside work around the place, while Mother took charge inside the main house. One of her worries was my brother Paul, age eight. He'd pop into the sickrooms where she was tending the houseful of patients, and nothing could keep him away.

Joe was sick two days before he gave in and went to bed. The flu ran its course, then pneumonia set in. But he passed the crisis and was doing all right, when Mother awoke to look at the clock one morning and saw that she had time for a short nap before it was time to give Joe his medicine. She dropped off to sleep and dreamed that Joe's heart would give way.

She awoke in a cold sweat. It was just six, time for Joe's medicine. She got up and went out to the annex. Joe lay in bed, white from the sickness, his pale skin contrasting to his glossy shock of curly black hair. He regarded her curiously as she entered. "Mother, what's wrong?"

"Time for your medicine. How do you feel this morning?"

"Pretty good. But you look like you've seen a ghost."

Mother phoned Uncle Fred and asked him to come right away. Uncle Fred, Father's younger brother, was our family doctor, and he never presented a bill. "John is trying to get to heaven with his family," he had told Mother years ago, in reference to my father's belief in the divine purpose of plural marriage, "and the least I can do is try to keep them healthy."

When Uncle Fred arrived, he examined Joe then went with Mother into the kitchen. As she closed the door, Mother broke down. "He's going, Fred! His heart is giving way!"

"The patient is all right. It's the nurse who has given

way," Uncle Fred said. "Nettie, you're the one who needs a doctor. You've been going night and day."

But Mother had been guided too many times for too many years. Nothing of importance had ever happened in her lifetime which she hadn't known beforehand. "His heart, Fred! His heart!" she exclaimed.

"I've examined the patient, and his heart is perfectly normal. But you need a sedative and a week's rest."

"With a houseful of sick people? I can't."

Two days later, Joe's heart began running wild. Uncle Fred prescribed whiskey as a sedative, but Utah was dry. All the prescription whiskey had long since gone from the drugstore shelves into highballs. It was impossible to fill a legitimate prescription in an emergency. Mother phoned every drugstore in Provo, then began calling Salt Lake. No whiskey could be had.

Next morning a pint flask was found tucked between the screen and the front door of the annex. Nothing was ever said, but we knew it came from Mr. Smith.

The medication was ineffective. Joe died three days later.

Mother was left alone now as she had never been before. Joe was her firstborn, and she had leaned upon him during the days of the underground and ever since. He had been her strength during the dark days of the Smoot Investigation, when her husband was offered as a sacrifice to the U.S. Senate to quiet the public clamor about Mormon polygamy. Joseph had grown into a manly man, so handsome it sometimes took her breath away, an athlete and a tiger in defense of the gospel. From the first weeks of his birth he had seemed to her almost too perfect for this world. Throughout his life she had resolutely put from her mind the gnawing presentiment that he *was* too good to last and the feeling had always haunted her that she should cherish him for the time that was allowed. Now he was gone at twenty-five, only three years after her husband had passed on. She felt very much alone.

A few weeks afterwards, Rae had a dream in which she had a talk with Joe. He told her not to mourn his passing, for he had been called to work with Father on a matter of great importance on the other side. Mother was comforted upon learning of the dream, but so quietly were such things taken in the family that Rae did not record the details of the dream until seventeen years later in a letter written at Mother's request. There was, for some of the family, a special affinity with forces of which most people are unaware.

Father knew before the event that he was to become an apostle of the Mormon church, and Raymond wrote a letter to Mother predicting that he would be called to the bishopric of his ward. "Well, it happened," he subsequently wrote, "right on schedule." Just as Mother knew by a dream that Rachel had become secretly engaged to be married while away teaching school and that Joe was going to die, so Rae knew of Joseph's death during the three days it took the telegram to reach the remote ranch at Ibapah.

With Joe gone, Mr. Smith was more than ever the head of the house. His two daughters, Mary and Helen, came again for summer vacation, and again Helen sat between my arms on the bicycle for mile after mile. When the railroad had a picnic at Lagoon, the pleasure resort near Salt Lake, that summer Mr. Smith invited us all as his guests. He went to the office to get passes, and the man said, "How many, Jim?"

Mr. Smith told him.

The man's jaw dropped. "What?"

"Jim's got friends," another man in line said, which certainly was true.

It was a big day for us: ice cream, pop, hot dogs, and enough dimes to take all the rides and play all the games. We coaxed Mother onto the roller coaster, and when the car reached the top of the first plunge she looked down at the terrifying abyss, screamed as the car dived into it, and assigned her soul to heaven. She lost all her hairpins while her long, auburn hair blew wildly as we flew around the curves. When she staggered off, with hair streaming, stockings dangling, looking like a survivor of a hurricane, we wondered if we'd gone a little too far with the practical joke. We knew it when she firmly forbade us to ever again ride the roller coaster, our favorite thrill.

Throughout the day Mr. Smith was there, the host, the man, the figure of authority. Curiously, that day was as close as I ever came to normal family life, as most kids know it. Father had loved outings, but they were always on a grand scale. There would be several wagon loads of family, and while it was great fun it was actually more like a club picnic or a convention than a family outing. But throughout this day we were a family just like other families. During this day Mr. Smith might have been our father. Never before had it been just our immediate family having a day of fun with an indulgent man in authority. And it never was again.

I don't know what might have transpired, except that soon after this there was a strike on the railroad. When it became apparent that the strike would be broken, Mr. Smith, a good union man, had to move on.

As he prepared to leave, he asked again for Mother's hand. Again she declined. That night a taxi driver brought him home and had to help him into the house. This was the first time in my life I had seen a drunken man, and the sodden face haunted me, the dead eyes unseeing in the red and wooden face.

Mother opened the door of Mr. Smith's room. "Take him in here," she said quietly. As the taxi driver helped Mr. Smith through the dining room and to the doorway of the bedroom, Mother asked, "Will he be all right?"

"Yes, Ma'am. He just needs to sleep it off."

Mr. Smith's dead and hopeless eyes looked slowly at Mother and then dropped away. If he knew anything at this point, it was that this was the end of a long campaign. Mother would have nothing to do with a man who tampered with alcohol, who arrived in the home in front of her children, helpless under its influence. This broke things off clean. He could leave now with nothing dangling.

Certainly Mr. Smith was not a drinking man. Certainly if he *had* gotten stinko, he could have taken a room at the Roberts Hotel for the night. Certainly he hadn't had to horrify Mother and the kids by parading his condition in the home.

He obviously had done it on purpose, knowing that nothing else could have broken things off for good and for all. Nothing else would have made it less painful for Mother to say good-bye forever. It was an act of sacrifice on his part, something which only a gentleman of the old school would have made. It was a grand gesture.

We never saw Mr. Smith again.

THE BOARDINGHOUSE KITCHEN

Mother's big kitchen attracted a wide array of interesting visitors, such as old Brother Carter who made salve. He had a long white beard, stained yellow around the mouth, his voice quavered, he walked with a cane, and he smelled bad. He loved to hear people tell him he really didn't look his eighty-one years, but to me he seemed a thousand. Once a month our kitchen served as the factory for his vile-smelling concoction as he boiled up a batch on Mother's range. She fixed him a hearty meal, which he ate with gusto, then he paid her with a little jar of his salve and carried the rest away to peddle from door to door.

Old Brother Koyle made soap. Old Brother Hutchinson made liniment. Old Brother Rogers made cough medicine. Our kitchen was not only the manufacturing center for their nostrums, but, since Mother never threw anything away, we kids were duly washed, dosed, and anointed with their products.

Then there were the old gentlemen who made gadgets which no household should be without. The inventors of these labor-saving devices were strong on tin cans and baling wire. Out of this they fashioned eggbeaters, tongs, can openers, potato peelers, flower baskets, and a hundred other very useful gizmos whose use only they could explain. Each arrived with his wire, cans, and tool kit periodically, set up shop on the kitchen porch, and manufactured a supply. Mother purchased every contraption that appeared at the back door, gave its inventor a good meal, and sent him away happy. Then she gave the dingus a look of puzzled dismay and put it in the storeroom. In time our storeroom was a veritable junk heap of weird gadgets fashioned by the submarginal fringe of Provo's entrepreneurs.

The bums also had the mark on our gate. Mother never turned away a hungry man. But having a fine sense of dignity, she never offered a free handout. She handed a hobo an axe or a digging fork and set him to work while she fixed the meal.

We kids used to claim that Mother took in her hard-earned money at the front door and threw it out the back. But she knew what insecurity meant. She knew what remote forces beyond control could do to plans and savings and position. She knew it as few did. And she had a soft spot in her heart for promoters, big or small. She had married one.

Old Brother Bean arrived one afternoon to use the kitchen for making his hair tonic. The stuff probably did no damage to the hair, despite its smell, but, being completely bald, Brother Bean wasn't the best person in the world to be its lone salesman. He explained this by noting that he had stumbled onto the secret too late to save his own thatch and his concern now was for others.

He also was concerned with financial backing. Brother Bean had the idea, common to the neighborhood, that Mother had a tidy sum salted away from her boarding business. A little arithmetic would have exploded this myth, but such stories thrive on lack of fact. Brother Bean was sure that fame and fortune would shower down, if only he had capital and a place to manufacture his product.

Mother had no intention of investing in the concoction, but found it difficult to tell the old gentleman so. He was a friend of long standing. In fact he had been associated with Father in Colorado, when Father was president of the mission there. Now Brother Bean had come upon hard times, and while she was always glad to let him use the kitchen for an afternoon and to cook him a good meal, she felt that was as far as her charity should go.

It was on one of these afternoons, with Brother Bean pressing Mother again to go into partnership, that the cat got shut in the oven. Sally was a gray-striped tabby, and she had hopped into the oven for a warm nap when the fire went down after dinner. When Mother began making up the fire for Brother Bean's tonic, she inadvertently shut the oven door, with Sally inside.

I came into the kitchen as Brother Bean was mixing his evil-smelling ingredients in a kettle on the stove. "Ah! Look at that hair!" he beamed, running his hand through my bushy thatch. "That shows what my tonic will do!"

"I find it very effective," Mother said, putting coal in the fire. She didn't add that she used it exclusively on Buttercup, our cow. The tonic was excellent for sore teats.

"With finance, we could have a fine, four-color label made up," Brother Bean said. "Your children—all of them with that wonderful curly hair—what a picture it would make!"

"My children—on the label of a hair tonic bottle?"

"A living testimonial! The picture alone would sell thousands of bottles!"

"I'm sure it would be a good investment for *somebody*," Mother said. "But I'm very busy taking care of a business of my own."

The stove was beginning to heat up, and Sally began plaintively mewing.

Brother Bean poured a black liquid into the witches' brew on the stove. "It would only take an hour or so in the afternoon, when there's nothing else to do."

Mother didn't want to injure the old gentleman's feelings by mentioning that this hour was the only one of a long day when she had an opportunity to sit down.

Lillian came in just then, wearing her Sunday dress. "How do I look, Mom?"

"Just fine, dear. Where are you going?"

"Only a matinee," Lillian said, almost too casually.

"Who are you going with?"

"Clyde," she said, a bit reluctantly.

"Clyde? Clyde who?"

"What's that cat mewing about?" Lillian asked.

"Never mind the cat. Clyde who?"

"Why, you know Clyde Roundy."

"Clyde—you mean, our *guest*?" Mother asked, horrified.

"Clyde's *not* a guest. He was only here a month, and that was a long time ago! Last year!"

"He *was* a guest," Mother said. To her, you might just as well try to change a leopard's spots as alter the status of a guest. "You know how I feel about going out with guests."

"It's only a matinee, Mother."

As the stove continued to warm up, Sally's mewing

took on an insistent note. "See if you can find that cat," Mother said. "And when Clyde comes, tell him I'd like a word with him."

"Oh, Mother!" Lillian complained, as she began looking for Sally.

"Do you realize, Sister Taylor, how many bald men there are in the United States?" Brother Bean said, stirring his brew at the stove. "There are *millions* of men losing their hair. If we only sold to one man in a thousand who needs our tonic, we would need to ship a carload a month."

Ruth came in, wearing a dress she was making. "I've got it basted, Mother, but you'll have to pin up the hem. And it ought to be given a couple of tucks at the waist."

"Samuel, see if you can find that cat," Mother said, as she began pinning up the hem of the skirt.

"Sounds like the poor thing's in pain," Ruth said.

I scouted around outside, on the kitchen porch, at the back of the house. Sometimes the yowling of the cat seemed to be one place, sometimes another. But Sally definitely was unhappy.

When I went back into the kitchen, Raymond and Paul had joined the group. The howling of the cat was loud now, and everybody was scurrying about. Paul was climbing the pantry shelves and Raymond was ransacking the storeroom. Ruth was rummaging among the pots and pans of the cupboards under the sink. Lillian was pawing through the junk in the closet of the kitchen porch. Mother was rushing about from place to place as the howls of the cat seemed to come first from one place, then another.

What with Mother's penchant for tucking treasures

away, there were a hundred places where the cat might have become trapped. I dashed outside for a stepladder when Mother became convinced the cat was caught in the attic, and as I brought it in she became equally convinced that it might be under the house.

At this juncture, Brother Snow and Brother Handley arrived. They were our ward teachers. "Good afternoon, Sister Taylor," Brother Snow said. "We just dropped by for our monthly visit."

"How nice of you to come," Mother said. "But things are a bit upset right now, so I'll just say hello and good-bye."

"But we find it so hard to find a time when you're not busy," Brother Handley said. "So now that we're here, we'll leave this month's lesson."

"But our cat's caught somewhere," Mother said. "I really don't—"

They filed into the kitchen permeated with Brother Bean's vile nostrum bubbling on the stove, while the cat howled and the family tore the place apart in search.

"The lesson this month," Brother Snow said, "is on the Word of Wisdom."

"How nice," Mother said, diving into the barrel of rug rags in the corner. "Ruth, look in the Hoosier cabinet!"

Ruth began casting pots, pans, odds and ends from the Hoosier as Brother Handley opened a hymn book. "Nothing we could say on the subject could compare with the immortal verses of Eliza R. Snow; hymn number 114, second verse—"

"Deli!" Mother cried, "look in the pantry shelves!"

Brother Handley read:

That our children may live long,
And be beautiful and strong,
Tea and coffee and tobacco they despise,
Drink no liquor and they eat
But a very little meat;
They are seeking to be great and good and wise.

At this juncture, Clyde Roundy arrived, having come around to the kitchen since nobody answered the dining room door. He had never been in the family portion of the house before, and the sight which met his eyes must have been somewhat unsettling. The place reeked with the brew Brother Bean was stirring on the stove. The cat was howling bloody murder. I was on a ladder throwing down things from the attic. Lillian was clawing through pots and pans under the sink. Raymond was heaving things through the doorway of the storeroom. Ruth was frantically cleaning out the Hoosier cabinet. Deli was throwing things from the pantry shelves. Mother was pawing through the barrel of rags, and the ward teachers were rendering the monthly lesson.

As Clyde looked about with bleak amazement, holding a box of chocolates in his hands, Paul rushed in with an axe.

"Here!" Mother cried, snatching the chocolates from Clyde and thrusting the axe into his hands. "Chop a hole in the floor!"

"Huh?" Clyde asked numbly.

"Right there!" Mother pointed to a spot before the stove. "The poor thing's caught under the house!"

Clyde looked about uncertainly. "Er—stand back."

Then as he raised the axe, Mother said, "Wait!" and slowly turned to the stove. Now that she looked at it, we all knew this was the source of the cat's howls.

"The oven!"

As I went toward it, Mother waved me back. "No, Samuel, you might get your eyes clawed out." She turned to Clyde. "Open the oven door."

"Me?" Clyde said.

"Hurry! Oh, the poor thing!"

Clyde advanced gingerly and grasped the handle. Then as the oven door opened, Sally literally exploded from the oven into his face.

We didn't see Sally for two days, and we never did see Clyde Roundy again. Mother was thankful that Sally wasn't really injured and was convinced that the incident was another proof that heaven was protecting her daughters from "the guests."

Nobody seemed to remember just what happened to the ward teachers when the cat exploded from the oven, and old Brother Bean, apparently convinced that Mother *was* too busy to become a partner in his hair tonic enterprise, never came back.

The chocolates were delicious.

CHAPTER 8

NEIGHBORS

What with family and guests, Mother's life was full. For years she had no time for outside activities. She never visited, nor was she neighborly. Good fences, she believed, made good neighbors, and eventually our lot was enclosed by what was practically the only remaining fence in Provo. For too long, in her early years, neighbors had been a menace, and even after the need for secrecy was gone she retained the habit of keeping strictly to herself and a circle of friends and family. She saw no reason to become chummy with anyone just because of the geographical happenstance of being neighbors.

When she was a child, a neighbor at Grantsville had become what the Mormons called a "skunk," hounding her father in an attempt to send him to prison for living with his plural wives. Later, when her own husband was in hiding because of plural marriage and a fugitive from a subpoena from the U. S. Senate during the Smoot Investigation, it was a neighbor, Ed Abbott, from Farmington who had doomed him by testimony in Washington. To Mother, neighbors would always be automatically suspect, particularly those who tried to be neighborly. It was an embarrassed neighbor who dropped in just to get acquainted and found Mother politely asking just what his business was.

One Provo neighbor had a singing hen. Clarissa was a barred Plymouth Rock, a fat and sassy hen that scratched around the backyard across the fence and was not confined to a pen. In the afternoon the neighbor would sit on the back porch with Clarissa in his lap and while stroking her on the neck would sing duets with her. I was entranced by Clarissa and watched from the fence while the neighbor and his hen harmonized.

"You'd think he would pen that chicken up," Mother said, when Clarissa got through the fence and began scratching in our garden.

"But, Mother," I said, "it's a trained hen. It sings."

"Annoying the whole neighborhood with its squawking. It really can't carry a tune." Mother seemed to feel that if a chicken sang at all, it should sing well.

"Clarissa is probably the only singing hen in the whole world!"

"Thank heaven for that," Mother said.

We were having supper a few days later when we heard the neighbor calling his hen. "Clarissa!" He rattled his can of corn. "Chick, chick, chick, Clarissa!"

"Listen to the fellow," Mother said. "Disturbing the peace. I do believe he's half rooster."

"Chick, chick, chick, Clarissa!" the neighbor called.

I enjoyed the duets and began slipping out the kitchen door.

"Samuel, finish your supper!"

"All done, Mom." I took what remained on my plate in my hand and ran out to the rear fence. I munched at the food while watching the man rattle his can of corn and call his hen.

Clarissa didn't come. "Don't understand it," the neighbor said, worried. He raised his voice, "Chick, chick, chick, Clarissa!" He shook the can of corn violently.

"Maybe somebody got away with her," I said. "Mom says that you ought to keep your chicken penned up. It's a wonder somebody hasn't caught Clarissa and cooked her."

The neighbor cringed at the thought. Clarissa was to him a personality and a pet. Then he looked at me, and his face slowly assumed an expression of surprise and horror. His eyes went round, his jaw slack.

"Boy," he croaked, "what have you got in your hand?"

I looked at what I'd brought from the table. It was a drumstick.

I was never articulate in a time of crisis and now I was stricken dumb. I knew that this was one of Mother's hens from our own coop. In fact, I'd beheaded the chicken personally, for Mother couldn't kill a chicken or bear the sight of the execution. But while my conscience was clear, I couldn't utter a word.

The neighbor clapped a hand over his mouth, whirled, and rushed into his house.

Clarissa was never seen again. I don't know what happened to her. And a short while later the neighbor moved away, possibly in an attempt to find a better environment. No doubt he spread the story to his new neighbors about how Mother had served her boarders the only singing hen in the world.

New neighbors moved in. The man of the house was a junk dealer, but with cultural aspirations. He practiced an hour a day on the clarinet and if that wasn't bad enough, it was summer, and he did his practicing on the back porch, just across the fence from our dining room. Worse than that, he did his practicing just at our supper hour. As the guests sat down at the table, the clarinet would begin across the fence.

What really made it hard to bear, however, was that the neighbor spent the entire hour every afternoon playing "Old Black Joe" by ear. That was apparently the limit of his musical ambition—to play "Old Black Joe" by ear—but having had no musical training, he always made the same mistakes in the same place, time after time, day after day, week after week, while our guests were at supper.

The guests began to mutter.

"If he'd only play something else."

"I wouldn't even mind "Old Black Joe" if he'd play it right. . . just once."

But he never played it right. The guests would tense for the mistakes that always came with mathematical precision.

"At least," Mother said, "the singing chicken didn't annoy the guests."

"Somebody ought to talk to him," Lillian suggested.

Mother considered this for a week or so. But, after all, it was the neighbor's own business, and she didn't want to interfere any more than she wanted to be interfered with.

Then at the end of the month, Mr. Murphy left. Mr. Murphy had been a guest for three years and was an excellent person. Mr. Murphy told Mother that he was being transferred to a new job out of town, but Mother learned that he hadn't been. He simply had moved to a new boarding house. True, Mr. Murphy had been of the nervous type and something of a musician himself. But still, Mother wasn't accustomed to losing out to the competition because of "Old Black Joe" being played badly.

Mr. Murphy's place at the table remained vacant. Under the circumstances, Mother didn't feel like letting a new guest enter the household.

The guests themselves finally decided upon a counter-measure. One afternoon when they sat down to supper they were all ready. As the neighbor finished stumbling through "Old Black Joe" the first time, there came to his ears through the open door of the dining room loud applause—clapping, whistling, and the stomping of feet.

The guests had a spy peeking through the curtains of the dining room window. "He's rattled," the spy reported, "embarrassed."

And then the spy's face fell as the neighbor, overwhelmed by the unaccustomed appreciation, gathered himself for an encore. Loud and firm came "Old Black Joe" played every bit as badly as usual.

From that time on, it was useless for Mother to protest. The junk man was happy in the fond delusion that he had an appreciative audience.

One evening Mother saw a notice in the Provo *Herald* that a quintet, consisting of string quartet and clarinet, was appearing on the lyceum program at BYU. Next day she put on her best dress and went to the university personally for a ticket. This was amazing to the members of the family, for she never went out in the evening except, as previously noted, to see *The Birth of a Nation* or a Harold Lloyd comedy. But what was more amazing was that on her return she turned in at the neighbor's house, introduced herself, and presented a pair of tickets to the junk man and his wife.

The next afternoon at supper time the junk man came onto his back porch and began the opening strains of "Old Black Joe." He came to his first mistake, paused, looked at the instrument in dismay, tried again, looked again, then arose and went into the house. Now he had heard a clarinet played right. And perhaps it was only a coincidence that the quintet, as an encore, had played ("By special request," it was announced) "Old Black Joe," beautifully and with variations.

The following afternoon the *Herald* carried a want ad: "Swap: clarinet for fishing tackle or what have you."

The junk man moved out when the house, which had been rental property, was sold to a new owner. Mother was happy at the news. Now, she declared, there would be some good, substantial, home-owning tenants. And the new owner proved to want as little to do with his neighbors as she did. This would have been fine with her, except for the situation of the common lane leading to the common barn which was half on one property and half on the other.

One morning the new owner received delivery of a wagonload of cedar posts. He went to work with pick, shovel, and crowbar, digging postholes down the property line. He put the cedar posts into the holes, and tamped the dirt well around them with the handle of the shovel.

"Nobody can get in or out with a rig or a car," Mother said with dismay. "How will we get hay to the barn for Buttercup?"

This, apparently, was her problem. The neighbor would make his own lane, and she could figure out her own solution.

The trouble was that he had space for a driveway along-side his house to the barn. We didn't. Even if we tore down the fence on our side of the lane, there wasn't room to get past the house, unless we tore off the porch. Then out behind the house was the bungalow, the Annex, which would have to be demolished for a driveway.

"Good fences make good neighbors," our neighbor said virtuously, stringing barbed wire on his cedar posts. "A common lane always means bad blood. I aim to get along with people."

Now, with his good-neighbor fence in, he surveyed the barn. It was a lovely barn, a great thing built half on his land and half on ours, the ridgepole exactly over the prop-erty line.

"It'll never work out," he declared, "people owning a barn together."

The fact that it *had* worked out, for half a century, made no difference to him.

I rushed into the house one morning. "Mom! He's tear-ing down the barn!"

Mother hurried out. The neighbor was attacking the barn with a sledgehammer and wrecking bar.

"See here!" Mother said. "We own half that barn!"

"Yes, Ma'am! I'm not going to touch *your* half!"

"But we have a cow. We need the barn."

"What you do with your half is your own business, Mrs. Taylor." The neighbor paused to deliver himself of his philosophy. "Anything owned in common is bound to cause a quarrel. Just like you coming out now when I'm minding my own business. I'm a peaceful man. I aim to get along with my neighbors." He picked up the sledge and gave a post a mighty swat and the barn shivered.

By nightfall, his half of the barn was demolished, sliced off at the ridgepole. What remained was a curious structure indeed, so I helped Raymond and Paul tear down our half. Mother then phoned an attorney about the barbed wire fence down the middle of the lane. The lawyer advised the neighbor that there was a legal easement over the common property.

At this, the neighbor took down the barbed wire, pulled up his cedar posts, put his place up for sale, and moved away.

"Like I always say," he declared in parting, "common ownership makes for trouble. A man tries to be a good neighbor and they put the law on him."

He moved onto a place out on the bench, where he could have a few acres for elbow room, and he could mind his own business without being bothered by neighbors. But we heard a while later that he got into a brawl with a neighbor about irrigation water and was severely beaten up when he threatened the neighbor with a shovel. Just downright unlucky, as you might say, in trying to mind his own business.

A woman with a swarm of thieving kids next moved into the house next door. On the day they moved in, Paul and I were constructing a shed to be used for storing flour, apples, and other supplies purchased once a year. We put down our tools and went in at noon for dinner. When we went out again the tools were gone. Hammers, saw, square, hatchet, level, and even the nails had vanished.

Full of wrath, I read the riot act to the new kids next door. "Just don't let me catch any of you little bastards on this property!" I yelled.

They scattered, but presently returned with their mother in tow. I expected her to apologize and return the tools, but she had another matter on her mind. Just who, she asked indignantly, was calling her children *bastards*?

I was nonplussed, for the term *bastard* had been used merely as an expletive, and had been one of the milder cusswords employed.

We had assumed that she was a widow, or divorced, because no husband was seen about the place. But the following spring, as the snow melted and the buds burst forth, a new baby toddled out of the house next door. While I was supposedly too young to know about such things, it became evident why she had been so sensitive to my language, as with each succeeding spring, another new neighbor wobbled into view.

CHAPTER 9

BONES IN THE WALL

Through the influence of Uncle Fred, one of the doctors who founded the Provo General Hospital, I went to work there when I got home after my year at Deep Creek with Rae and Clarence. The very first day on the job I unearthed a human foot, blackened by gangrene, in the vegetable garden. This gave an exciting prospect for interesting work, but the task of helping with the lawns and garden never fully lived up to its early promise.

However, I must confess that for an eleven-year-old there is nothing quite so fascinating as medical journals, with their candid accounts of incredible subjects and their eye-popping illustrations. Many an hour the lawn hoses remained unmoved and the weeds thrived in the garden while I was holed up in a basement or attic. The insulation of my plastic mind smoked from the voltage of gripping and illustrated accounts of disease, surgery, abnormalities, or sexual problems. My newfound sophistication made the prattling by my peers about sex, always a lively topic among boys, seem childish in the extreme.

My brother Paul came to work with me the following summer when the hospital got a flock of chickens. The job was steady, full-time in summer and part- time during the winter, the school year coinciding with the period when the lawns and vegetables didn't need tending. Two evenings a week we mopped the lower floor of the central hospital building, which contained the doctors' offices and operating room. Every afternoon the chickens had to be fed. Uncle Fred lived next door, and we did daily chores for him as well. He matched the institution's monthly check of ten dollars with a like amount of his own.

A vital item of the chickens' diet, Uncle Fred told Paul and me, was the bonemeal made from the huge joints that came from the hospital kitchen. But preparing it proved almost too much for our strength, and eventually, alas, our integrity.

Grinding the bones was a nightmare. The machine had a heavy flywheel, on which was a wooden handle for turning. Uncle Fred, demonstrating the grinder, turned the flywheel rapidly, and the cutters shaved the bones handily. But Paul and I weren't strong enough to get the flywheel going with much momentum. We struggled with it, pushing it around slowly like the handle of an ice cream freezer when the ice cream starts getting hard. After fighting it for twenty-five revolutions I'd rest, panting, while Paul took his turn. It took an hour of the hardest kind of work, every afternoon, grinding those infernal bones.

It was on Christmas Eve that things reached a climax. It had snowed the day before and turned bitter cold. I was shivering out in the carriage house as I measured out the sacked feed for the chickens, while Paul went with the coaster wagon for the scraps from the hospital kitchen. He returned with the two cans on the wagon, looking not only cold, but bleak. The bone can was half-full of short ribs, and, in addition, there was a huge joint.

Looking at the enormous joint, Paul said, "I didn't know they served elephants to the patients."

We put the short ribs into the grinder and began turning the big flywheel.

"It'll take two hours, at least."

We wanted to go Christmas shopping. Paul's nose was blue and my toes tingled with cold.

"If the ground wasn't froze solid, we could bury the big one," Paul said. We giggled at this.

Finally the short ribs were ground and I opened the machine to put in the big joint. Then I looked up to see Paul atop the bench. The bench was against the end partition, which stopped a couple of feet short of the ceiling. Paul stood on tiptoe upon the bench, reaching up with the joint bone, holding it with both hands atop the partition.

"What if I dropped it down between?"

We burst into laughter at the thought. It was preposterous. Paul laughed so hard that he lost his grip. The big bone, slick from the soup kettle, slipped from his hands. It clattered down between the studs of the partition and thumped hollowly at the bottom. It was gone; there was no getting it back. Tittering guiltily, we hastily fed the chickens and raced away on our bicycles to do the Christmas shopping.

While this first time was an accident, the second wasn't. For awhile, it was just those great joints that clattered down between the sheathing of the partition. But before long it became all bones, while the grinder stood idle, and, guilt ridden, we lived in terror of discovery.

With spring, the buds began bursting and a strange odor began permeating the carriage house. Every time Uncle Fred would drop in, he'd sniff and declare that we'd have to keep the place spic and span. We tried to, but there was no getting at the source of the odor, short of ripping the partition boards off and cleaning out the pile of bones between the walls.

I was raking the lawn beside the east building of the hospital one day when somebody called my name from the second story. It was Clug Varney, a school classmate. I went up to his hospital ward, which was on what once had been a large screened porch, now glassed in. Clug occupied one of eight beds in the ward.

"What you doing here, Clug?"

"Dad was going to surprise Mom with a piano for her birthday and it fell on me while I was helping him get it up the steps." His right leg was in traction.

We chatted a few minutes, and a nurse came in with lunch for the ward—scrambled eggs, toast, mashed potatoes, corn, stewed peaches, coffee for the adults, and milk for Clug.

"What do you do for the hospital?" Clug asked me.

"Oh, work on the lawns and garden, and feed the chickens. Those eggs come from the hens I feed," I said proudly.

"Best eggs I ever et!" a man in an adjoining bed chimed in emphatically. "What do you feed 'em, kid?"

"Mostly stuff from the hospital," I said. "Scraps, meat, bones. Then we get sacked feed—"

"Wait a minute," the man said. "What was that you said—bones?"

"Oh, yes," I said, hoping the guilt wouldn't show on my face as I remembered how we were cheating on the bones. "We grind up the bones for the chickens."

"Grind up the bones for the chickens," the man said, looking at the scrambled eggs in his plate. Suddenly he put a hand to his mouth.

"Nurse!" Clug cried, "Mr. Whitehead is going to be sick!"

As the nurse rushed to help Mr. Whitehead, another man said, "I don't believe I'm hungry, after all."

"Why the hell does that kid have to come up here at mealtime?" another man demanded. "Feeding bones to the chickens!"

"Perhaps you'd better go, Sam," the nurse told me.

"Come back later!" Clug called as I went out.

I was completely mystified about the uproar until I saw Clug the following afternoon. "Don't talk about feeding bones to the chickens," he whispered to me. "You see, Mr. Whitehead had his leg amputated."

At that moment I realized why the people in the ward had suddenly lost their appetite. "Oh, but they're not human—"

"Shh!" Clug warned.

I was never much at explanations and I never did try again to put Clug straight. But the rumor got out that the hospital was grinding up human bones for the chickens. I have wondered if this was a factor in the decision of the hospital to go out of the chicken business shortly thereafter.

Years later I was talking to an old carpenter, and he told me that he'd heard the hospital utilized amputations by feeding both flesh and bone to the chickens. "But don't you believe it," he said. "I was remodeling that old carriage house and found out where they used to put the bones—down between the walls. One partition was full of 'em."

While Paul and I still feel guilty about those bones, we never had the slightest twinge of conscience about blowing the fuses of the hospital electrical system, which might have been serious. When the mood came upon us, we would unscrew a light bulb, insert the face of a small hammer into the socket, and glory in the magnificent hissing and sparking. When one socket went dead, we'd scout around down in the storeroom or out in the carriage house until we found another live one, then blow it, too.

As we went, hammer in hand, searching for more fireworks, we'd hear somebody call out, "It's that X-ray machine again!"

The hospital called in an electrician. He was known as Coke and had started life as a bicycle repairman until the automobile brought about a change of vocation. He checked the X-ray machine, the appliances in the laboratory, the outlet plugs, and the bed lamps. Everything checked out, but when he was gone the fuses would start blowing again. He was called in again and once more made a thorough examination.

"Circuits overloaded," Coke said.

"We didn't have any trouble until we got the new X-ray machine. Why don't you look at it again?"

"I've looked at it again. Nothing wrong with your X-ray machine, except it's the last straw," Coke said. "You got to modernize your wiring. This place started out as three homes, just places for families to live. So you converted them into a hospital, patch here, add there. That old wiring—it's a wonder you ain't burned the joint down long ago."

"Can't you patch it up once more?"

Grumbling, Coke tried again, but the next day he was back when more fuses blew.

After several weeks of this, they called Coke in for a last time. "Look here, a hospital *has* to have reliable wiring. If you modernize it, will it be dependable?"

"I guarantee it," Coke said.

They gave him the go-ahead, and he modernized the wiring.

"Now she's safe," he said. "She'll give you no more trouble."

And he was right. By that time, Paul and I were tired of the hammer trick and occupied with other challenges. And it probably did no harm for the wiring to be modernized.

One day while climbing around in the rafters of the carriage house I looked between a couple of boards making up the ceiling and discovered an absolutely wonderful thing—a secret room. It occupied a cupola on the roof, and when I had squirmed past the false ceiling and into it, I found that it was outfitted with a couple of benches, some old books, a little table, and even a miniature deck of cards.

Presently I heard Paul come into the carriage house.

"Sam?" he called.

"Upstairs!"

His feet thumped on the wooden stairs, then stopped as he reached the barren loft.

"Sam? Where are you?"

"Downstairs!"

His feet thumped down the stairs.

"Where'd you go to, Sam?"

"Upstairs!"

Then as he came up again I began laughing, and he located the sound of my voice as being overhead. "Up on the roof? How'd you get up there?"

I peeked out from the false ceiling. "Climb up this post and you'll *really* see something!"

Paul's eyes went round with wonder as he crawled past the false ceiling into the secret room. This was absolutely a dream come true for any kid. A hideaway. It had been made years ago, when the carriage house was part of the property of a private residence, before the three big homes had been converted into the hospital. Uncle Fred didn't know anything about it; nobody did except just us two.

Blowing the fuses was nothing, compared to having a secret room. We loved to be up there, playing poker with matchsticks, when Brother White came into the place looking for us.

Brother White was the yardman for the hospital and our immediate boss. He was a genial old gentleman, plump, red-faced, and with a great white moustache. Paul and I took advantage of his good nature by playing pranks on him, one of these being to put a bucket of water over the door to fall onto him when he entered. Either our engineering was wrong, or a hallowed legend is based on a false premise, because we never did catch him with the water over the door. We tried dozens of times, with the bucket balanced in various ways, but it just didn't work. The water came either before he entered or after he'd gone through the door.

We decided to take direct action, and one afternoon when Brother White came into the carriage house to tend the furnace in the basement, we were perched atop the partition into which we dropped the bones. I had a bucket of water and Paul had a bucket of garbage from the kitchen. As Brother White opened the door, we both let him have it.

As he sputtered and let out a roar of rage, we realized that we'd gone too far.

We hopped off the partition onto the bench. Brother White roared around the partition and through the doorway of the room as Paul dived out the window into the chicken yard. There was no time for me to follow. I sprang from the bench and raced out the back door of the room, with Brother White in pursuit. I ran along the hallway and bounded upstairs. Then I knew I was trapped. There was no place to escape, no exit except the stairs I'd come up, and Brother White was stomping up them in pursuit.

I shinnied up the pole like a monkey and into the secret room. Through a crack I saw Brother White pause at the top of the stairs and survey the loft.

"Now then, boy! We'll teach you a thing or two. Enough's enough! Come out of where you're hiding or I'll come after you!"

I remained deathly still in the room overhead.

"Sam!" he roared. "Come here to me!"

I made no answer, and he set his jaw. "All right, I'm coming and it will be harder on you!"

He began moving through the loft, looking behind boxes and various objects put there in storage, keeping a sharp lookout to make sure I didn't spring from behind something and break for the stairs.

When he reached the end of the loft he paused, looking about, puzzled. I had to be there, but I wasn't. Just then a breeze rattled the big doors at the end of the loft, that formerly were used to allow hay to be pitched in. Brother White gaped at the doors, his anger changing to concern.

"Oh, dear," he breathed. He opened one side of the doors and looked down apprehensively from the loft to the hard earth below.

"Sam!" he quavered. "Are you hurt?"

At that instant some perverse imp inside me caused me to utter a moan. It was as if a knife stabbed Brother White.

"Oh, the poor boy," he muttered, as he hurried across the loft toward the stairs. "Maybe sprained an ankle."

At this, I emitted a louder moan. Brother White gasped. "Or broke a leg! They went too far—but they're only kids, after all."

He clattered downstairs. "Sam!" he called as he hurried around the building to the rear. "Where are you, boy? Are you hurt bad?"

I let him search awhile down there, and then I gave vent to a great and quivering moan. From below came Brother White's gasp. He hurried around to the front and clumped up the stairs. By the time he reached the loft he was gasping. He'd lost his hat, and his snow-white hair was awry. Sweat was running down his face. His great moustache quivered. He began searching among the things stored in the loft again. "Sam! Don't hide, boy! You needn't be afraid of me. . . ! Oh, what will I ever tell Dr. Taylor—I chased the boy into jumping out of the loft. . . Sam, where are you?"

Quite obviously if I'd injured myself jumping out of the loft, I couldn't be hiding now in the loft, but Brother White was too agitated for logic.

One more moan, I thought, would really fix him up good. So I put everything I had into it. But perhaps I tried too hard, for halfway through my voice broke, and what began as a moan ended as a wild laugh.

Brother White stiffened. He looked about the loft slowly. "You little devil," he said. Then he began to chuckle and from the secret room I joined in and we roared together.

CHAPTER 10

LEAN YEARS

Mr. Allport, boss of the spinning and carding departments at the Knight Woolen Mill, was short, muscular, and
so heavy that he was almost square. He took down my
name and address, then said, "And you're sixteen."

I said nothing. I was fourteen and small for my age.
Mother had bundled me into a sheepskin coat several sizes
too big to make me appear older. Mr. Allport, a neighbor
and friend, probably was aware of my age, but he didn't
know. At sixteen I was legally of age to work around dan-
gerous machinery, of which the great room at the mill was
filled. Gears were without covers. Overhead shafts drove
the enormous drums of the carding machines with heavy
belts which were slid on and off the huge driving and
idling pulleys by hand. Floors were slick with oil.

Shortly after I began work, there was an accident in the
rag-picking department. Chuck, who ran the rag-picking
machine, used to sit with us during lunch break. He was
eighteen and was taking organ lessons, with the ambition
to someday play the great pipe organ for the Mormon
Tabernacle Choir. The rag-picker ground up strips of discarded woolen goods—sweaters, coats, blankets, whatever.
Chuck put the stuff onto a belt which fed the material

through rollers to a drum whose spikes chewed it into shoddy. One day a strip of goods was suddenly snatched through the rollers and a loop of it caught his hand. We heard his screams through the wall as the spikes chewed off his fingers, his hand, and up his arm. We arrived to find Chuck unconscious, his arm off to the shoulder.

When he got out of the hospital, Chuck called around at lunch break to say hello and good-bye. With the settlement from the mill he was going east to study music. I suppose he ended up teaching music, composing or conducting it, but I don't know; we never heard of him again. The accident became the basis for an early story I wrote about an old man working in a mill whose young granddaughter needed an operation which the family couldn't afford (no Medicare in those days). He caught his hand in the rag-picker, and the settlement financed the operation. He didn't lose the arm; he gave it.

I worked in both the spinning and carding departments, helping the spinners take the full bobbins off the mules which spun and wound the yarn, put on empty ones, weigh the yarn, and credit it to their piecework accounts. I filled the hoppers of the cards from the wool bins, took off the big spools containing twenty ends, put on empty spools and stacked the full ones on racks.

When a lot of one color of wool was changed to a lot of another color, we ran the belts off the overhead driving wheel and the pulley on the card, dismantled the card, and stripped it with hand cards. It was a trick getting the belt onto the overhead wheel again and then onto the enormous pulley that drove the card. We swabbed a length of belt with water, then flipped it onto the overhead wheel, holding it steady as the water made it slick, then we adroitly ran it onto the lower pulley by hand. Somehow, nobody got hurt in this operation.

Working hours were from four to ten P.M. after school, and from seven A.M. to ten P.M. during summer vacation. Saturday, however, was a short day, only seven A.M. to six P.M. On Sunday we caught up on our sleep. I earned the princely wage of seventeen and one-half cents an hour. When, after a year, I was raised to thirty cents, I felt rich, and along the way I did learn the trade. Spinning was the top job at the mill. If you could run a mule, as the spinning equipment was called, you could find work anywhere.

But I always knew the mill work was only a temporary necessity. The other wage slaves, both men and women, carried lunch buckets with a thermos of hot cocoa or coffee, I brown-bagged it. The lunch pail was the badge of the working stiff. I was going to be an author. I hadn't yet written anything for publication, but I knew I was going to.

One day the mill caught fire. Fortunately, the fire department was directly across the street. Unfortunately, the firemen charged through the carding room with their hose to get at the blaze, which was in another department. They knocked over the rack of carding spools, jerked down the wires of the overhead feeders, smashed windows, chopped down a door rather than opening it with the knob. They did make short work of the fire, but long work for us repairing the damages.

My career in the mills included a stint at the Pioneer-Pacific Worsted Company at Long Beach and a summer at the mill in Santa Ana. My mother allowed me to go because we needed the money, and because I could live with my sister Deli in Santa Ana. The Long Beach operation was curiously strict. Promptly at seven A.M. doors were locked and work began. If you were two minutes late you had to enter through the office. It soon became apparent to me why the entire operation was so nervous. Worsted material is a high quality product, made from long-fiber wool. This mill was using short-fiber wool, and in fact, mixing in a bit of shoddy stuff as well. I don't know who blew the whistle, but one day a man climbed the ladder to the high water tank, painted out the word *Worsted* and painted in *Woolen*. From then on, the doors weren't locked during working hours.

At the Long Beach operation I lost my taste for cherry pie. Each morning a girl came through the plant selling Bluebird box lunches. The other men in the spinning room cast the inevitable cherry pie into the waste basket and ate the remainder of their lunches. For awhile I enjoyed three or four discarded cherry pies for my lunch. Finally I became as tired of them as the other men and I tossed mine into the wastebasket too. I haven't eaten cherry pie since.

Shorty, who ran a mule in the same aisle as mine, was the best spinner I ever knew. He could pick up and join eight broken ends, before the mule arrived to wind the yarn onto the bobbins. I fancied myself pretty good, but four was my limit. We helped each other, and made something of a record. All was peaches and cream, except that my brand new mule was cantankerous. For no apparent reason it would run out, begin spinning, then suddenly charge in with a horrible crash, bending heavy steel rods like hairpins. Clem, the mule fixer, would fiddle with it, straighten out the rods, and the mule would work for a few days, then bang, another crash.

Shorty diagnosed the trouble. There was a slipping set-screw on a worm gear which regulated the timing mechanism. When the set-screw slipped, the machine crashed.

"I'm the mule fixer!" Clem roared when Shorty tried to tell him to tighten the set-screw. "Git lost! Buzz off!" Mule fixers were jealous of their secrets. No spinner could hang around and watch them work, let alone offer advice. "Git you ass outta here!" Clem cried. He spoke with a dialect I'd never heard before: "I don't like he," he would say about the office manager, "He too stuck up, and he wife she the same way."

Clem and the spinning boss, though, were great pals. Every Saturday night they got drunk and bought the favors of a hooker.

My mule continued to self-destruct, however, so Shorty and I watched our chance. When Clem and the boss left the spinning room together, I shut off my mule and Shorty raced to Clem's tool kit, grabbed an Allen wrench, raced back, gave a tug at the set-screw, and from then on the mule was gentle as a lamb.

At Long Beach I went swimming in the surf every day except one. On that day a cop stopped me for indecent exposure on the public streets. I was wearing pants and shoes, but the cop ordered me to go back and put on a shirt, or else. At that time men's swimming suits had tops. How times have changed.

One day I swam out quite a distance, then was waiting for a big wave to ride in, when the riptide brought a pretty girl alongside me. "Please help me," she pleaded. "I'm drowning."

I held her head above water. "Take it easy. You'll be okay.

Just relax. I'll hold onto you, and we'll let the big breakers take us in."

As the big one rushed at us, I said, "Take a deep breath and hold it. I'll hang onto you. Don't panic." The breaker knocked us tumbling about in the foam. When we surfaced we were several rods closer to shore.

"That was fun, wasn't it?" I said to reassure her. "Take it easy and get your breath while we wait for another big one." Within a few minutes I touched bottom, and we had it made. I studiously avoided staring at her breasts, which had popped out of the suit, as she blushingly tucked them back inside. Then she thanked me.

"No problem," I said, "I save girls all the time." She was pretty, she was grateful; but a bashful teenager lacked the courage to ask her name or phone number. I never saw her again.

The Pike at Long Beach paralleled the beach, offering a permanent sideshow carnival. There was the man with all his joints frozen: "Roy! Roy! Slowly turning to stone alive!" Barefoot messiahs paraded with homemade banners proclaiming the end was near. Queers, not gays in those days, infested the public rest room, propositioning me. A man we called "the basket case" could dress himself and roll cigarettes, although he had no arms or legs. He sold pictures of himself with his wife and children. The "spit-and-argue" club held forth at the Pine Avenue pier, where—astrology, numerology, dowsing, perpetual motion, electrical healing, and the evils of wearing colored clothing or buttons—were vehemently argued, and no argument was ever won or lost.

The mill I worked at in Santa Ana had its own cast of characters. Pop was the oldest worker at the Santa Ana mill.

He must have been fifty, incredibly ancient to me, and he'd worked in woolen mills all over the country for thirty-odd years. His career terminated abruptly when he ran his hand through a set of gears. They led him away with what remained of the hand dangling to the floor.

I visited him in the hospital. "I was going to quit anyhow at the end of the month," he said. "Guess I stayed one day too long." He and his wife had made a deal to take over a mom-and-pop grocery from an old couple who were retiring. Pop was fitted with a clever metal hook device, and soon was doing okay at the grocery.

Another worker, Bob became rich when a wealthy uncle died leaving Bob as sole heir. We congratulated him as he shook hands all around, saying good-bye. No more mill work for him. Three days later he showed up ten minutes before starting time, driving a brand new Oakland car and wearing a three-piece suit. He joined the wage slaves sitting on the porch chewing the fat while waiting for the day's work to begin. He showed up again at noon to eat a box lunch along with us and chat. Mill work was all Bob knew and mill people were his only friends. When I left in the fall for BYU, Bob was still coming twice a day to visit with his pals.

It was while working at the Santa Ana mill that I ruined the acting career of my sister Deli's husband, Harry, by arriving at their home in Santa Monica with two blankets from the mill as gifts. The blankets weren't to blame, but rather the fact that Harry, a film extra, went out with me that evening for a jar of fig jam. While we were out, Central Casting called. Harry wasn't there, and another extra got the part. He became convinced that this stymied his career. However, it might just as easily have been the time when he was sitting by the phone one day, with Deli at work, and two men arrived.

"Where is it, buster?" they ordered.

"Where's what?" Harry wanted to know.

They trussed him up and ransacked the apartment. Finding nothing, they left, and then the phone started ringing, but Harry couldn't answer. He learned later the caller *had* been Central Casting.

Harry's story did have a happy ending, however. Instead of being an extra waiting by the phone, he became the genial gateman at Columbia Studios on a first-name basis with stars and executives, a job he loved.

It was also the Santa Ana mill that saw my rise to power and fall from grace in the milling world. I became night boss of spinning and carding. Eager to make a record the very first night, I was raking the accumulated lint from under a card with a bamboo rake without shutting the machine down. The sharp teeth of the enormous cylinder caught a tine and pulled the rake through the works, with a spectacular display of flying parts. The day boss, Ern Arrowsmith, covered for me, saying the card had caught up a hunk of lint. But truth crushed to earth will rise again, and I was demoted to running a mule on the day shift.

Though I never again ran a mule after my Santa Ana days, I treasured my skill as an ace in the hole. If I struck out as a writer, I knew I could get a job anywhere as a spinner. Then I heard the dismaying news that progress had eliminated the iron mule in the woolen business so it would be root, hog, or die as an author.

I had one more memorable summer job during my high school years. I spent my next summer as a teenager in Salt Lake with widowed Aunt Ellen, my father's sixth wife, while working at the Baldwin Radio plant in East Mill Creek, where Aunt Ellen was secretary. I worked in the magnet-filing department. The magnets were circular, encasing a coil, and had to be filed just so. It didn't take me long to learn that applying assembly-line tactics—doing each operation to all the magnets, then the following operation to all—I could increase my production. In fact, I was so prolific that during the slack season, the 40-odd men in the department were all laid off except three, and I was one of the three they kept.

Those were summers of a bygone era. After work I'd often walk the mile or so to Highland Drive, grab a streetcar to town for a big night, taking in a movie, buying a magazine, and/or standing with the men on a corner watching the girls in short skirts get on and off the streetcars. On one such expedition I picked up a copy of a new magazine, *Liberty*, with a cartoon on the cover showing it marching with the two big weeklies, *Collier's* and *The Saturday Evening Post*. I hadn't published anything yet, but I just knew I'd be in all three of them. My literary ambition at the time was to write a book about filing magnets—I wasn't thinking much about sales.

People sang "Among My Souvenirs"and "My Blue Heaven" in those days, and of course the latest Irving Berlin tune, "Blue Skies" and his earlier classics "Always" and "All Alone." Charles A. Lindberg thrilled us by flying the Atlantic; Babe Ruth, Sultan of Swat, hit 60 homers; Hollywood awarded the first Oscars; the Mormon prize-

fighter Jack Dempsey lost the heavyweight title to Gene
Tunney with the disputed "long count"; and CBS began
broadcasting the Salt Lake Tabernacle Choir.

The Kellogg-Briand Anti-War Pact forecast an era of peace
in the world, with fifteen nations signing an agreement.
From a plethora of cartoon shorts emerged two prominent
characters: the raffish rabbit, Bugs Bunny, and the remarkable rodent, Mickey Mouse. Walt Disney was on his way to
fame and fortune. And Clara Bow was the *It* girl of films.

When I began high school in Provo, in between all those
summer jobs, more than half the cars in America used the
same ignition key, and all were the same color—anything
you wanted so long as it was black. As I remember, Henry
Ford's Model T cost $245. This was the basic model. If you
wanted luxury items such as a battery, self-starter, top and
windshield, the tab was $310. This was a time of flappers,
short skirts, flagpole sitters, bathtub gin and speakeasies; of
Aimee McPherson's Four Square Gospel and Fatty
Arbuckles's *Brewster's Millions*, of John Gilbert, Renee
Adoree, Rudolph Valentino, and Sinclair Lewis.

Professional wowsers toured Mormon country during
my years at Provo High. As defined by H. L. Mencken,
who was my ideal at that time, a wowser was a redneck
haunted by the fear that somebody, somewhere, might be
happy. These zealots dedicated their lives to terrifying me
and my peers regarding what, in those simple days, were
the two major threats to Zion's youth: the cigarette habit
and the "solitary vice." A cigarette meant tobacco, not a
joint of Maryjane, while alcohol, drugs, and teenage preg-
nancy evidently were problems of the wicked outside
world, not the kids in my valley.

At this time cigarettes were called coffin nails, and a standard attraction among the Freaks of Nature exhibits at carnival sideshows was the Cigarette Fiend, a pitiful specimen of humanity puffing a half-dozen coffin nails simultaneously. Thus, we dubbed one wowser preaching against the evils of tobacco the cigarette fiend. He asked for four volunteers from the audience, then opened a cardboard box and took out an alley cat. As four huskies from the football squad each held a paw, the fiend injected a nicotine solution from a cigarette into the cat. My sympathies were all for the cat, which yowled pitifully, writhing and twisting in agony before subsiding as the poison took effect. I wasn't impressed, knowing that various foreign substances—milk, for example—would have the same effect if injected. The lecture was wasted on me, anyhow, because after smoking for seven years I'd quit at the age of twelve for fear it might stunt my growth. (Alas, too late; I remained the runt of the litter.) I felt only outrage at the callous brutality of the cigarette fiend who, as the huskies held the poor cat, thundered the warning that cigarettes were the devil's kindling wood that would lead to a life of dissipation—liquor, loose women, social disease, the gutter, and early death.

And then in the midst of this tirade, the cat began to revive. As it gained strength the four assistants were jerked about as they struggled to subdue it. One claw came free, and it slashed at the other three hands. The cat dropped to the floor of the podium and bounced as if on springs as the four huskies and the cigarette fiend sought cover. The cat bounded onto the lectern, then with a mighty leap sailed through a window, while the auditorium rocked with cheers.

The sex maniac, as we called the sin-stomper who preached against the "solitary vice," threatened debility, nervous collapse, loss of memory, pimples, rotting of the moral fiber, insanity, eternal damnation, and hair in the palm. He pointed dramatically to the eastern mountains, where the Utah State Mental Asylum marked the end of Center Street. There, he thundered, was the end of the line for the pitiful victims of the pernicious habit.

Another wowser who toured the lecture circuit when I was a teenager was the flag phony. I sat with the student body of the Provo High School and local citizenry in the Provo Tabernacle while the flag phony went on and on and on about Old Glory. I was sure this guy was as phony as a three-dollar bill, and I was reminded of Samuel Johnson's statement that "Patriotism is the last refuge of the scoundrel."

At the climax of his tirade, the flag phony bellowed, "Is there anyone here who wouldn't take off his hat when the flag is passing by? If so, stand up and be counted!"

I stood up, which set him back on his heels. Obviously, this never had happened before. "Young man, why shouldn't you take off your hat when the flag is passing by?" he demanded.

"Because," I said truthfully, "I don't wear a hat."

This brought a roar of laughter, and he had no reply. At that time, everyone wore a hat—boys and girls, men and women. I didn't for the reason that the standard hat size stopped at 7-1/2, while I took 7-3/4. I was the only person in Provo who didn't wear a hat.

I never did find a hat to fit me until I was drafted into the military during World War II. At the induction center we were issued uniforms. The supply sergeant asked, "What size hat do you wear?"

"The biggest one you've got."

With a grin he produced an oversized hat which he used to rib rookies with small heads. It fit perfectly. I wore it until I was commissioned an officer. As a lieutenant I would have no trouble finding hats which fit, no doubt because, as any GI will attest, all officers had the "big head."

CHAPTER 11

BECOMING A WRITER

My first accepted manuscript had come upon graduation from high school. I was a writer! But I had enough sense to realize that I needed more education. What with all the night work at the mills, however, I lacked sufficient credits to enter college. So I wrote a paper on the operation of woolen mills, which was accepted for extra credit, enabling me to enroll as a freshman at BYU. Brigham Young University had 1,500 students during my tenure, and there was a persistent rumor that the Church was going to give it back to the Indians. When my daughter enrolled, many years later, she was one of some 25,000 students.

During my sophomore year at BYU, a girl named Gay Dimick had won the Elsie C. Carroll Gold Medal for the prize Christmas story. Gay Dimick also wrote other things of local note. I had been trying to meet the talented author, but in vain. There had been a Miss Dimick in a course I took in commercial law, but this vivacious redhead proved to be Georgia, Gay's sister. I knew Dan Dimick, for he and all his pals from southern Idaho stayed at the hotel where I worked at the beginning of a new term while looking for more permanent quarters. They all registered under the same name, Joe Budro, until Budro became something of a local character, his comings and goings duly noted in the

My ever-loving wife, Gay

Provo Herald. Dan was Gay's brother. But where was the talented Gay?

The obvious answer to my quest was to ask Georgia or Dan, but this possibility never dawned on me. I continued the search.

During the summer following my junior year at BYU, I became desk clerk at the Roberts Hotel, from six A.M. to six P.M. My brother Paul took the graveyard shift. On my first day on the job I found Ida Dusenberry, my kindergarten teacher, sitting in the lobby. Our eyes met and held in recognition. She had stayed at the Roberts for several years, in a small room which rented for five dollars a week. Soon after I became night clerk she checked out, and I never saw her again. Was it me?

I wore several hats at the Roberts: cafe cashier, bouncer, switchboard operator, and bellhop. I also mopped the lobby and kept the books. I filled the Iron Fireman with coal for the furnace, and I tried to keep hookers out of the place. When school began in the fall, I took the night clerk position, six P.M. to midnight, and in my spare time I hit the school books. After all, I was taking a full course load at dear old BYU. I was also learning the power of the press by writing a column for the school paper, the *Y News*.

For my work at the hotel six hours a night, seven days a week, I received the princely stipend of thirty dollars a month, another thirty dollars for keeping the books, plus ten dollars for typing the daily cafe menu. Perks included one hot meal a day and the privilege of raiding the cold room for a midnight snack. Tips provided pocket change. I was lucky to have a job. The depression was on, and freight trains were lined with men looking for work.

Busy as I was, I somehow found time to drop in at the public library each month to absorb the immortal gripes of H. L. Mencken in the *American Mercury.* Also, by tending to the bulletin board in the lobby which listed the movies, I was given a free pass. Since I worked seven nights a week, I went to matinees. I saw the silent movies of Viola Dana, Buster Keaton, Fatty Arbuckle, and such landmark films as Chaplin's *The Kid* and Harold Lloyd's *Safety Last.* John Gilbert was the big star until Al Jolson ushered in the talkies with *The Jazz Singer.* Fatty Arbuckle rivaled Charlie Chaplin in popularity until a girl died at one of his wild parties.

For awhile the "Amos and Andy" radio show became so popular it threatened to bankrupt the town's three movie palaces. Spellbound listeners refused to leave their radio sets of an evening to attend the movies. The managers of the Strand, Princess, and Columbia finally decided to join rather than fight the competition. In the middle of a gripping movie the screen would suddenly go blank, and the audience would be regaled with the Amos and Andy radio program. Even though I got in free, I resented this violation of a man's right to choose his own entertainment, and complained in my column for the college paper.

While gaining a liberal education in the humanities at college, I also received a liberal course in human nature at the hotel. I'd always accepted the premise that all was well in Zion, but as a hotel clerk, the facts of life dashed some of the dew from my innocent eyes. Even among the fairest flowers of Zion, I discovered, love would find a way—generally via the back stairs. I tried to keep the back door locked, but the key had entered the public domain, making it impossible to keep that door fastened. One of my duties was supposed to be keeping the hotel free of hanky panky, but it was easier said than done. By and large, the salesmen who crowded the hotel Monday nights—their first stop out of Salt Lake—were a decent lot. However, a Mr. R. continued to have a girl in his room every Monday night, and he'd boast about it the next morning. The manager, Mark Anderson, said, "Sam, anything you can do to discourage that character, go ahead. We don't want that kind of business."

Next Monday night I rang his room. "This is the desk. Please keep your door open when a girl is in your room."

"Why don't you mind your own damned business?"

I checked the room. Door shut. I rang again, again, again, again. Finally he stormed downstairs. "Okay, you bastard! Step outside!"

We went out under the corner streetlight. He aimed a wild haymaker at my head. I blocked it and gave him a left to the nose. I'd done considerable boxing, but this was my first and only fight without gloves. He was furious, and bigger, but a sucker for a left jab. After I broke his nose he said, "Okay, buster, but you've lost a steady customer. This is my last night in your fleabag."

"Thanks a million."

His nose was a sight next morning when he checked out.

"Good work, Sam," Mark Anderson said, "and good riddance."

When it came time for closing the books for the year at the Roberts Hotel, I ran into a problem. I was dealing with two corporations, one the hotel, the other the cafe, and I'd never tried keeping a set of books before. There were also the income tax returns to make out, another first for me.

To prepare, I'd enrolled in an accounting class at the Y, and I'd secured a mail-order book, *Bookkeeping Made Easy*, yet I really hadn't mastered all there was to know about it.

One day at school when there was a column of figures to add for the accounting class I walked into Dean Hoyt's anteroom and asked the pretty secretary if I could use the adding machine. She said go ahead. I did, then asked her name.

"Gay Dimick," she told me.

"Gay Dimick! I've been looking for you for three years!"

With that for openers, it took only five more years to con her into marriage.

What with my "spare time" work of 42 hours a week, dating Gay Dimick, writing "Taylored Topics" for the *Y News* and short stories that occasionally appeared in the pulp magazines, I admittedly wasn't a straight-A student at the Y. However, during my four years I flunked only two courses. One I walked away from; the other resulted from what I considered a humorous item in "Taylored Topics" which ruffled the sensibilities of a faculty member.

The noble experiment of prohibition had made drinking fashionable, and the bootlegger became a quasi-respectable figure. As night clerk I discovered that several BYU students were working their way through school as bootleggers, which was newsworthy enough in my mind to mention in the column I wrote for the student paper. The ink was hardly dry on the *Y News* before I was on the carpet. When I refused to name the suspected bootleggers, I was suspended. After I was reinstated, the next column picked off the scab, and I was out again. The pattern repeated itself until after the sixth suspension I had been tied in the closet once too often. I dropped out. After all, I can take a hint.

Besides, who needed a degree? I was an author, publishing in national magazines, albeit infrequently. But who was I kidding? For several years I had a recurring dream of going back for my degree, only to be thwarted.

Later, upon being drafted in World War II and going overseas, I had no more dreams of trying to get my degree. When you're enjoying each day as it comes because there might not be a tomorrow, you have other things to dream about. Still, it hasn't been easy professionally, having no degree. When I was invited to chair a session at the annual meeting of the Mormon History Association, I listed on the form that my institutional affiliation was "The University of Hard Knocks." More than fifty papers were given at thirty-one sessions, and of all the authors, all the commentators, and all the chairs, I alone had no "institutional affiliation."

Upon dropping out of college during my senior year, I also quit my desk clerk job at the Roberts. The hotel management wanted me to continue keeping the books. The thirty dollars a month plus one good meal a day would guarantee survival during those dark days of the Depression, when World War I veterans in uniform and wearing medals stood on street corners selling apples at five cents apiece. But, I turned the job down, not wanting security to sap my initiative. It was going to be sink or swim as a writer.

Being a "pro" now, I sent my next story, with a five-dollar fee, to a critic who advertised in *Writer's Digest*. When his criticism arrived I shot off a furious reply, informing him that he was crazy. In return he said that I'd better do the story in my own sweet way, which advice was worth the five dollars. And the end of *that* story is that a pulp magazine bought the yarn I wrote—in my own sweet way.

A writer needs an office—not a "studio." Behind our house was a little shack we called the sleeping porch, with walls boarded halfway up and screen above. I filled in the upper half, leaving windows, installed a little pot-bellied stove, bought an old roll-top desk for three dollars, and was now in business. This would be the first of three offices, the second being at Palo Alto, the third where I am writing this now, at Redwood City, California.

There are so few full-time pros in the writing business that, outside the fraternity, I simply never talk about it. Many times people have asked, on discovering that I am an author, "Yes, but what do you do for a living?" With people who knew me as a golfer, I said, "publicity" when asked what I did. One word sufficed. With neighbors, however, it was another matter. "Poor Mrs. Taylor," they said, "married to this lazy bum with no visible means of support. He disappears into his shack in the morning, appears once in awhile, looking into the sky as he wanders down to the mailbox and back. What *does* he do for a living?"

And then, I discovered, they had the answer: "He's an airplane watcher. He works for the government." Okay, if that satisfied them, so be it.

I followed *the Girl* to California, a writer can live anywhere, while my new wife wouldn't consider being lost in the horde of Taylors in Provo, where in the Bay area I found, to my vast surprise, that by and large, gentiles were remarkably like Mormons—mostly good people with human foibles and conceits, with an occasional rotten apple in the barrel. Here, I was no longer a member of a dominant ethnic group. Mormons were few and far between in California at that time. The first known Mormon in

Redwood City, J.D. Clark, arrived in 1925. In 1927, the San Francisco Stake was organized. It consisted of ten wards in San Francisco and, across the Bay, in the Oakland area. The remainder of California was a mission. When I arrived, during the Depression, no services were being held in Redwood City; members attended Palo Alto Ward, five miles away.

When I wasn't writing out in California, I was busy being married and building a house. In the midst of this, I became acquainted with a Turkish student attending Stanford: Kenan, who was bedazzled by the charms of my wife's younger sister. Kenan was incredulous that a professional author should also be a carpenter, electrician, plumber, tile-layer, roofer, and handyman. He wanted to help, to learn American ways. However, as a member of the Turkish upper class he never in his life had held a tool in his hands. I literally had to show him which end of the hammer to take hold of. He couldn't drive a nail, saw a board, use a square, or adjust a pipe wrench. It was incredible watching him awkwardly trying to shovel dirt or push a wheelbarrow. I worked on the house for three years, by which time Kenan learned as much on the job with me as he did at Stanford. On returning to his native land, however, he didn't take my wife's sister with him, nor did he ever again hold a tool in his hand. This remained part of his memory of youthful days, to be recalled each Christmas in the letters he wrote my sister-in-law, year after year.

Among my friends in the writing business, Albert Richard Wetjen was the most successful. He was the author of sea stories for *The Saturday Evening Post* and *Colliers* at the time—the very best market for writers in the world. He came to Utah with me to be on the program of the Annual Roundup of the League of Utah Writers. Whenever we stopped to visit a member of my family, construction was under way. Raymond was building an eight-unit apartment house; Ruth had just finished a rental apartment in her basement; Lillian had added a new living room and bathroom; my mother had lowered her old-fashioned high ceilings. I didn't recognize Paul's house because it had changed so much since I'd seen it a year previously.

"Sam," Wetjen said, "at last I understand you."

A reputation as a handyman does have a definite point of diminishing returns. I became one of the most unpopular men of the San Francisco Peninsula as wives nagged husbands—"Why can't you fix things like Sam does?" Wanda Price, wife of E. Hoffmann Price, the king of pulp adventure writers, heckled him about the badly-fitting front screen door to the point that he purchased two fine handsaws, rip and crosscut, then invited me to dinner and to fix the screen door. I fit the screen with his saws, together with a tool kit I'd brought along—plane, square, screwdrivers, hammer, nail set, wood chisels, breast drill, center punch, and so on (you can never tell just what you'll run into). With the right equipment, it proved a simple job.

"Ducky," Edgar Price said to Wanda, "I'd hate to tell you what these two saws cost, and they're only the beginning. Take a gander at Sam's tool kit," whereupon he wrapped his saws in waxed paper, put them in a closet, and never used them again.

Ironically, in the midst of the current do-it-yourself craze, I don't rate at all. When I laid bricks for a patio, I was asked, "Did you make your own bricks?" Merely *laying* them was beneath notice. One homemade power tool in my workshop was so photogenic—a combination jigsaw, post drill, sander, grinder, and polisher—that it appeared in a Walt Disney movie. But I no longer qualify as a craftsman; I'm a jack-of-all-trades eccentric.

I've even become quaint as a writer. When asked, "Do you use a word processor?" I must reply, "I *am* a word processor."

CHAPTER 12

THE LAST GOOD WAR

My ever-loving wife forwarded a letter from Walt Disney to me at the 176th Ordnance Depot Co., Ft. Lewis, Washington, during my first week of basic training. It wasn't uncommon for men in their thirties to be drafted at that time. I was thirty-six.

What had interested Walt Disney in hiring me were stories I had written for *Liberty* magazine. One was about eccentric Professor Rhoades, who had invented a synthetic rubber which would cure the wartime rubber shortage. He mixed up some stuff in a beaker, poured it in with the gas of his Model T Ford, started the engine, then caught the rubber as it dripped from the exhaust pipe. It was a superior product, much better than natural rubber, but with one minor defect—when dropped it bounced slightly higher than it fell. The professor put some on his heels and began bouncing up and down, higher and higher. He had a hell of a time figuring out how to get down. Another story was about Professor Rhoades and his gizmo to repeal the law of gravity. This time he took his flying Model T Ford for a ride.

A month previously I gladly would have given my right eye for the opportunity to work for Disney Studios, and I could have been exempt from the draft if Walt had mailed that letter then, since he produced war films. Still, it really didn't bother me to inform Disney that I was fully employed by the Army of the United States for the duration. In fact, there was a certain patriotic satisfaction in making the sacrifice for the war effort.

In basic training I was a one hundred percent eager-beaver rookie: hut-hoot-heet-hoer; close order drill; qualifying with the .30-06 and the carbine; making up my bunk until a dime dropped on it bounced; bivouacing under camouflage conditions, pup tents pitched on eight inches of moist mulch under dripping conifers, while weapons carriers worked night and day carrying men off to the hospital with pneumonia. As we huddled damp and bone-chilled in the mess tent at night, we sang, "You Are My Sunshine." The training films were entirely lost on us. The minute the lights went out, we fell asleep. Each morning there was a long list on sick call. In the supply room, where I worked, an entire wall was stacked with the barracks bags belonging to men in the hospital.

I survived bivouac; I made the 30-mile forced march under full field pack, though I was twice the age of the fuzz-faced 18-year-olds. Basic training was to weed out the weaklings. Old man or not, I survived.

My eager-beaver attitude lasted several weeks. Then one night near the end of my basic training I couldn't sleep. It was around midnight when I got up, dressed, and went to the orderly room preoccupied. Ignoring the man on guard duty there, I passed through to the supply room, where I had access to a typewriter. A story had been growing within me; now it was ready for delivery, and I had to give it birth.

By morning I had it written, with the manuscript in an envelope.

It was another fantasy for *Liberty*, about a Superman-type character named Captain Comet who was drafted into the Army. He could do everything the comic book Superman could do—the flying through the air, feats of superhuman strength, and so on—but he had problems. The night flying was hell on his sinuses, so he wore long johns underneath the natty Captain Comet costume his wife had stitched up for him. He also was completely frustrated professionally. As he flew out night after night, he never did meet up with Superman, Batman, Spiderman, or other confreres, nor could he find any mad scientists plotting against the world, any evil invaders from outer space, or beautiful girls in jeopardy.

In the Army, Captain Comet was a misfit. He was called Goof-Up. There simply wasn't a place in the Table of Organization for a Superman.

As I dropped the manuscript in the mailbox, I realized that I really wasn't a soldier at all. I was a writer, and I'd been doing research. For the next two and a half years I took a detached view of the Army of the United States as a civilian in uniform.

After boot camp, I was sent to Salt Lake City for officers' training in the ASTP program, only to discover upon arrival that the ASTP had been scrubbed, so it was to be ten days of close-order drill before returning to my company. Always looking for an interesting story, I got an overnight pass while I was still in Salt Lake and interviewed ex-Mormon Bishop Koyle, who for some forty-odd years had been operating the Dream Mine near Spanish Fork without finding any ore. But he knew he would eventually strike it rich because he claimed heavenly visitors had taken him inside the mountain one night and showed the ore to him. During the depths of the Great Depression he had built a magnificent mill, gleaming white on the mountainside, to process the ore when it should be found. He financed the operation by selling stock to believers in the dream. I sat up all night to write the story, which went to *Esquire*.

I was overseas when the story appeared. My brother Raymond reported that LDS Church officials said it was the best thing written to prove that Koyle was a fraud and a swindler, while the dreamers considered it the best thing ever written to prove the authenticity of Koyle's heavenly visitation. One thing for sure, Koyle told a convincing story. Each week there was a new sign that riches were near, but to my knowledge the mine never produced.

Soon, my unit became part of the 5,000 troops jam packed aboard the British liner *Andes,* en route to England. The CO of our outfit told Phil Watson and me to contribute a story about the 176th Ordnance Depot Co. to the ship's paper. Phil was a reporter from the San Jose *Mercury* and I wrote magazine stories. We improved on the idea by compiling a glossary of nautical terms for the edification of the GI landlubbers:

> bow: sound made by puppy which has only half learned how to bark.
> knots: fasteners, as square reef, clove hitch, bowline.
> hawser: GI's reply to an officer's joke.
> port: A red wine.
> hold: wrestling term, as hammerlock, half-Nelson.
> wharf: sound made by puppy after it becomes a mastiff.

steer: a neutered bull.

wheel: to manipulate, as wheel and deal.

wake: to cease sleeping.

mast: british for *must, most,* or *missed.*

deck: to knock someone down. Also, to deck out.

bridge: dental appliance available only to officers.

dock: to subtract from wages.

keel: head over heels. To keel over.

rail: to complain.

companionway: arrangement between friends.

bulkhead: a blockhead or numbskull.

We also told of a ship's captain who had a paper in his locker which he would often take out, scrutinize, then lock up. One day he neglected to fasten the locker, and the first mate examined the paper. It said, "Port, left. Starboard, Right."

The captain and first mate wasted no love on each other. The captain reported in the ship's log: "The first mate came aboard drunk." When the first mate was on watch, he recorded, "The captain came aboard sober."

The GIs enjoyed our items in the ship's paper. But the CO of the 176th Ordnance Depot Co. was not amused.

In Europe, I transferred from the by-the-numbers Ordnance outfit to the Air Force Public Relations Office (PRO) in London, where the informality was a welcome change of climate. On reporting, I shook hands with the colonel and other officers, rather than saluting. Colonel Max Boyd told me that my first assignment was to write a book about the fighter plane pilots, in collaboration with Captain Eric Friedheim. Then he turned me over to Sergeant Dorfman for briefing.

"Here's your 'Correspondent' patch for the right shoulder," Dorfman said. The insignia read Correspondent, U.S. Army. "Get Air Force insignia from the supply room and cut the stripes off your sleeves," he continued.

"Okay, but why?"

"You'll be interviewing officers, and you won't want the master race calling you 'corporal.' I'll fix up your permanent travel orders for anywhere in Europe," he said. "Go find yourself quarters for when you're in town."

"But what about the notice on the bulletin board which says that all enlisted personnel must report to the barracks, no exceptions?"

"Ignore it," Dorfman said. "We're professionals here. Colonel Boyd is a veteran Associated Press man; Lieutenant Colonel Ben Lyon of Radio Section is an old movie actor—married to former star Bebe Daniels—and big in British radio. Major Arthur Gordon of the Magazine Section, where you are, was editor of *Cosmopolitan.* Captain Eric Friedheim was a feature writer. You don't want to be in the barracks—bed check, roll call, KP, guard duty, CQ, hut-hoot-heet-hoer!"

As a result, I didn't meet my first sergeant or commanding officer of Headquarters Co. for six months. And I fought the war with my own weapon—a typewriter.

After my first assigned book, *Fighters Up,* was completed, my next assignment was to ghost the annual "Report of the Commanding General of the U.S. Strategic Air Forces in Europe to the Secretary of War." I never saw the general; he was at the Pentagon. For this job I was furnished with a general's staff car and driver. And let me tell you when that car with a star on the license plate arrived at a base the guards waved us through with style. Then out of this car stepped a GI without a single stripe on his sleeves. But, in effect, my orders carried the authority of four stars, and I received full cooperation.

It's a long way through channels from the London PRO to the Pentagon, but the report suffered no damage. Evidently the general liked my prose, for I was tapped for the job the next year.

I continued writing magazine stories during the war, as well. Inasmuch as we were on duty seven days a week, I wrote a story only when I had to. An idea would grow within me like a baby developing, until I had to deliver it by sitting up all night. Let me say that writing is more than a craft, more than an art. It is a disease. Remember "Captain Comet," my first story in uniform, was written at night on the supply room typewriter. *Liberty* published it. The next was born when moving off maneuvers at Bend, Oregon. I checked in equipment for 280 men and at the same time typed out a 5,000-word story. Then at Camp Shanks, New York, the Port of Embarkation for the European Theater of War, I began writing a story on the pay typewriter in the day room. The machine worked for a half hour per dime. The line grew behind me, GI's waiting to write home, but I was writing a short story and couldn't quit. When my five dimes were exhausted, the machine froze in the middle of a big scene. I asked the others for a dime; I offered a quarter, four-bits, a dollar for a dime. No dice.

So I went back to the barracks and continued writing with a fountain pen. At ten, lights went out. I went to the only place where the lights were on all night and sat at the only place there was to sit. My fountain pen ran dry, and I continued with a pencil. By morning I had the story written, which I smuggled out past censorship to my New York agent (I dropped it in a mailbox off the post). And so it went for the next two years overseas.

So I offer my love and heartfelt sympathy to any of you who suffer from the writing disease. But if you have got to have an ailment, I can't imagine a better one.

At the liberation of Paris I was highly pregnant with a hell of a story, and I delivered the baby that night. I put the script on the secretary's desk with a note, "Elsie, please type this up and send to my agent."

Next morning we flew nineteen civilian correspondents to Paris, including Ernest Hemingway, Mary Welch (a pretty correspondent for *Time* whom Hemingway later married), Demaree Bess of *The Saturday Evening Post*, Drew Middleton of the *New York Times*, and others. Not knowing what to expect, we included field tables, folding cots, blankets, C-rations, lanterns, whatever, in our cargo. But to our happy surprise we found ourselves billeted at the Ritz Hotel that night. Next morning we sat at tables with snowy tablecloths, fine china, and gleaming silverware. A procession of waiters marched in with tureens. We had arranged with the hotel to exchange ten-in-one rations— the best Army field chow—to supplement the local food, and we anticipated a gourmet delight such as only the French could provide.

The waiters uncovered the tureens and set before us cans of C-rations, which were edible only in dire extremity. The ten-in-ones hadn't arrived, and after years of German occupation, the French were wary of promises.

Major Al Paris of our office made the classic observation: "Camping at the Ritz."

By lunchtime the ten-in-ones had arrived, and we enjoyed fine French cuisine.

Soon after returning to London, I received a V-mail from my agent: "The Post liked the horse story." The Post, of course, was *The Saturday Evening Post.*

Horse story? What horse story? I asked Elsie, "Was the story I wrote before going to Paris about a horse?"

"Oh, yes indeed, and very funny."

"Did you keep a carbon?"

"You didn't tell me to, did you?"

The baby had been delivered, and completely forgotten. So I tried to reconstruct the story in my mind. I had it figured out before I received a copy of the magazine.

Andy Rooney was on the staff of *The Stars and Stripes.* From him I learned that I was known as the "Hollywood writer." Not because I had written for Hollywood, which I hadn't, but because of the perks for GIs at the USSTAF—no barracks, no drill, no bed check, availability of aircraft, permanent travel orders—what a life!

About this time though, after six months of freedom, Headquarters Company finally cornered us by cutting us off at the pockets. No more could Sergeant Dorfman pick up our pay. We had to report, in person, or no scratch. So we trudged over to the orderly room, where the first sergeant, with extreme sarcasm, pretended great delight at meeting us. "So this is Corporal Taylor!" he exclaimed. "How glad I am that you could spare the time to drop by and get acquainted!"

He then introduced us to the CO, Captain Fogarty, who

gave it to us, by the numbers. We would report to barracks before bed check at ten, no excuses. We would draw KP and guard duty. We would fall out at six for roll call and close-order drill.

"And that," he said, "is an order!"

It was a bedraggled bunch of writers who wended our way back to the office. "It's a shame, men," Colonel Boyd said, "treating you like GIs. Wish I could do something about it. But—" He finished with a shrug.

"Colonel, I've got an idea," Fuller said. Fuller was the greatest operator I ever met, and the PRO was full of them.

"Don't tell me, Fuller," the colonel said. "I don't want to know."

When I arrived at barracks with my shaving kit shortly before ten that night, the operators were in action. They had hauled a field table into the barracks, typewriters, a mimeograph machine, a teletype, a radio transmitter.

"What is all this stuff?" the CQ in charge of quarters asked.

"We've got to get out a communique by midnight," Fuller said.

"All I know is lights go out in three minutes."

"Okay, if you want to take the responsibility. Major sir," Fuller said into the transmitter, "there's a CQ here who's holding up the general's speech!"

"Get that man's name, rank, and serial number!" the reply crackled. It came, of course, from our radio truck.

"We'll see about this," the CQ growled and vanished. Presently he returned with the top kick and the captain. They stormed in as the operation was going full blast, the radio blaring with the general's speech, typewriters clicking, the operators bandying big-time shop talk, while the men trying to sleep in the barracks griped about the lights and the racket.

"What the hell's going on here?" the captain demanded.

"Direct order, sir. Report to barracks."

"Clear this stuff out of here! We've got thirty men here trying to sleep!"

"Yes, sir!" Fuller said, then into the radio: "Major, Captain Fogarty here won't allow us to work, we won't be able to get out the general's speech."

"Now, wait a minute, soldier," the captain said. "Why didn't you tell me you had work to do tonight?"

"That's the nature of PRO work, sir. Meanwhile, we've got to get out a communique about the general's speech before midnight. And, sir, while you're here, we've got to get the teletype hooked up in the morning, and we'll need a couple of phones, including a scrambler."

"Can't you finish this work back in your office?"

"Oh, yes sir, but you ordered us to barracks."

"Okay, I'm ordering you *out* of barracks," the captain said. "And don't come back!"

I returned to my apartment at Queen's Gardens, and we had no more trouble from Headquarters Company.

Fuller's scheme was worthy of a medal, and though he didn't receive one for this dodge, the PRO did garner its share of recognition. Nine members of the PRO were awarded the Bronze Star Medal for services above and beyond the call of duty. We all piled into a jeep and sped through the streets for the presentation ceremony. We didn't get far when an MP pulled us over. "Only four personnel allowed per jeep," he said.

"But we're heroes," we explained. "We're on our way to be decorated by the general."

"Okay," he said, "but five of you heroes climb out of that jeep."

Five of us heroes managed to arrive in time by taxi.

The Legion of Merit was tougher to come by. It was difficult to get, particularly for a GI, but Colonel Boyd thought I should have it for *Fighters Up,* the Pentagon reports, and such, and he assigned an officer to write the commendation. When headquarters kicked it back, Colonel Boyd handed it to me. "Sam, can you fix this up? Give it some zonk."

So, with some embarrassment, I began revising my own commendation. Fortunately, Maurice Barrangon, another top-notch writer who had made his way into the PRO, volunteered to help. Between us, I qualified for the Legion of Merit, awarded in recognition for outstanding services above and beyond the call of duty. And that, friends, is how I became a war hero.

As the Germans retreated we followed, setting up press camps for correspondents in mansions in cities taken by allied forces. The owners of these houses were only too happy for us to occupy them because in the chaos there was promiscuous looting, particularly of big houses owned by the wealthy. Everything was taken including, literally, the kitchen sink! Light fixtures were torn from ceilings, hardware from doors, toilets pried from bathrooms, wash basins and medicine cabinets ripped out, drapes torn down, carpets torn up—everything taken except books. In walking through a looted house you waded ankle-deep through books and papers. The libraries of the wealthy

actually were of much greater value than the bathroom fixtures, but looters aren't usually of a literary bent.

When following the front lines, we stayed as close to the
action as was safe for the correspondents. The question at
times was a matter of knowing where the front was. Once
we overshot the mark. At Regensburg we entered the city
before it was captured, commandeered a mansion, and set
up a press camp. That night there was a furious battle, and
by morning we were in Allied territory.

Another time, Major Clark Newlin, reconnoitering in a
jeep, suddenly found himself rolling through a German
encampment. The Germans, as surprised as Newlin was,
gaped as the American jeep passed through camp. Newlin
waved and smiled. Pete, his driver, when telling about it,
spread his arms: "My back felt *this* wide!"

We were usually transported by air. When taking off and
landing at bombed airstrips in overloaded C-47's stacked
waist high with loot in the aisle between the bucket seats,
we had to be ready to spring up if the copilot called,
"Everybody to the front, so we'll clear the fence!" Under
such conditions, it was easy to tell new arrivals from the ZI
(Zone of the Interior, the USA). They sat there beaming
and relaxed. Those of us who had been lucky too many
times always carried a mystery paperback in a rear pocket.
As the engines gunned for the takeoff, out came the paperback. When airborne, and high enough for safety, the
paperback went back in the pocket, to be pulled out again
at landing. I carried the same paperback for a year and half,
and never did read past the first chapter.

With Europe overcast much of the time, a good deal of
the flying was by instruments. But one day with a cloudless

sky I was in a C-47 which had lost the door to the pilot's compartment. The pilot and copilot were examining a map. The pilot pointed to the left. The copilot shook his head and pointed right. And *these* were guys I entrusted my life to in bad weather? I never did trust airplanes anyhow. In my opinion, the world would have been spared much trouble if the mother of the Wright brothers had used birth control.

In London, the battle between the PRO and the censors of S-2 downstairs was just as real as the air war between our Air Force and the Luftwaffs. Colonel Max Boyd was dedicated to telling the simple truth. S-2 wanted nothing said at all. "You fellows," an S-2 officer told me, "are the best friends Jerry has" ("Jerry" was slang for the enemy). The other side of the coin was that it was vitally important to maintain the credibility of our communiques.

When we lost more than 200 heavy bombers in an attack on the ball bearing factories at Schweinfurt, Colonel Boyd wanted to report the facts, appalling as they were. However, Wedewing (headquarters for all publicity) ruled otherwise, so we tried to apportion the losses a few at a time in reports of other bombing attacks. But truth persists, and more than twenty years later I met a historian who, on hearing of my positions at USSTAF PRO, said, with a curled lip, "You lied about Schweinfurt, didn't you?"

The S-2 stops were posted on our bulletin board. They included a release from General Eisenhower's headquarters. As a public relations project, the general gave a blood transfusion to a GI—a nice enough human interest story if you didn't stop to wonder if the supreme commander didn't have more important things to do. Anyhow, the story was released, complete with art, when the GI died. Let me tell you, there was a scramble killing that piece.

Another choice story concerned a member of a bomber crew who on three occasions leaped from a disabled plane without a parachute, before it crashed. Each time he landed on a grassy slope and was none the worse for the experience. S-2 stopped the story because the Air Force didn't approve of leaping from aircraft without a parachute.

My greatest personal victory over S-2 was to slip a top secret map past them. In ascending order, classified materials are "restricted," "confidential," "secret," and "top secret." I got the square S-2 stamp on the map, allowing publication, but when it appeared in color, on the cover of the Army magazine *Yank*, the egg hit the fan. They couldn't get back at me because I *had* submitted it to S-2, but I will admit that I didn't get much past them from that time on. In fact, on a subsequent story a husky MP with a gun at his hip arrived at my desk to demand the manuscript and pictures. I didn't argue with him, but of course I kept a carbon. After the war, I published the story.

With all PRO personnel on permanent travel orders, and Paris just an hour and twenty minutes away, some of the office "operators" got rich. The hottest item was the Mickey Mouse wristwatch, which sold for about 10 shillings at the PX. A PRO photographer did a land-office business in Germany, trading Mickey Mouse watches straight across for Rollie twin-lens reflex cameras, which he sold in London at the bargain rate of 10 pounds.

While I never was an operator, I had Fuller and the other smart cookies at the PRO blinking with awe and amazement when I pulled off the biggest promotion of all—a trip to the ZI. Traffic was all the other way, of course. *Nobody* went back. But I actually went to New York for ten days, to talk with editors. Of course Gay met me there. Though I'd been overseas only a year and a half, with a war on I'd forgotten little things. For example I asked her, "Do you play the piano?"

And ah, the food in New York! After eighteen months of powdered chow, I was hollow inside. So it was oyster and clam cocktails, crab louie, fresh eggs, and milk shakes three times a day for my ten-day stay.

On one of my last evenings in New York, Gay and I had an Italian dinner at a little cafe. When I paid the check the manager said, "Roosevelt's dead." He put his finger to his lips, "Shhh."

Bereft people poured into the streets. Times Square was jammed. A newspaper photographer lined up a shot of a soldier, a sailor, and a marine reading the headline, "FDR DEAD!"

"What they won't do for a story," a man muttered disgustedly. "Why, if Jesus Christ returned to earth, they'd make a story out of it!" Indeed they would, in Second Coming type!

Uniforms were few and far between in New York. With my three overseas Hershey bars, my ribbons—Legion of Merit, Bronze Star Medal, ETO ribbon (European Theater of Operations) with three battle stars—I received royal treatment. To conserve gasoline, the taxi cabs were loaded with people going to different addresses. I couldn't pay a fare; when I got out, somebody had already paid. At the cafeterias it was dry toast for breakfast, because civilians couldn't buy any butter, because it had all "gone to war."

but when they saw the uniform waitresses whispered, "The butter's underneath."

When my time in New York was up, I kissed Gay good-bye and went to Bolling Field to fly back. I was out of cigarettes. "No cigarettes, Mac," the man at the counter said. Then he asked, "Where you going?"

"London."

"*London?* How many cartons do you want, Mac?"

Regarding smoking, practically everyone in uniform had the habit. I didn't smoke before being drafted, not since I was twelve, but bought a pack of cigarettes at the induction center. We all figured that if we were going to be cannon fodder, to hell with taking care of our health. When I got home after the war I quit the habit, cold turkey.

Only two men of the 176th Ordnance Depot Company didn't smoke. One was a Jehovah's Witness. The other was Barney, a fellow Mormon who had served two missions. He also was permanent latrine orderly because he refused to work on Sundays, and we were fighting a seven-day-a-week war.

Barney also refused to touch Army coffee. Overseas, the only safe water available was disinfected, foul-tasting stuff from Lister bags. Barney would just scoop up a canteen from any creek, utter a quick prayer to kill the bugs, and drink. He was never sick a day during my time in the company.

As for myself, I considered Army coffee too feeble to be sinful.

Back in England the war was getting hotter by the minute. From the Pas de Calias, a town on the coast opposite London, Jerry harassed London with buzz bombs and rockers, the V-1 and V-2. S-2 informed us that Grosvenor

Square, our center of operations, was the primary target. While they missed us, it wasn't by much. The British put up a screen of cables tethered to barrage balloons to catch the buzz bombs, but many bombs got through anyway. Nothing stopped the V-2.

First warning of an approaching buzz bomb was the undulating wail of sirens, followed by three bells of the PRO buzzer. We'd go out into the hallway while the hollow drumming throb of the bomber's engine increased in volume, sounding like the old four-cylinder Dodge of my childhood. Then as the throb reached a crescendo overhead, it suddenly cut off. The robot now was circling silently, descending, to hit *where?* We stood against the wall, away from the brass railing of the stairwell, waiting for the explosion. Sometimes it was just a heavy, dull grunt; at other times, a sharp slap on the ears, hard enough to make my head ache. Once when a bomb hit nearby in Hyde Park, the house shook. A half hour later bits of leaves from the park trees floated down past our windows. On another day, a formation of our troops in a nearby street took a direct hit.

The daylight attacks were irregular, but you could set your watch by the nightly assault, which began at eleven. As a harassing tactic, it was highly effective. A number of people in the PRO simply had to get out of London every night. Others became philosophical and lived with it. I stayed in town. One night the windows of my room were shattered, but that bomb still didn't have my number on it. After shaking the glass off the blanket, I went back to sleep.

The V-2 rocket came without warning. Just a slight swish for perhaps a second, then an enormous bang. It seemed that this should have been a worse psychological threat than the buzz bombs, but it wasn't. If you heard the bang, you were okay. If you didn't, you had nothing to worry about. As a terror weapon, the V-2 was a fizzle.

One night after a poker game at the office, Pete Robinson, Buzz Lawrence, and I were walking along Oxford street near Marble Arch when Pete yelled, pointing at the sky. Here came one. Three GIs hit the pavement, as the V-2 struck a nearby pub. We visited the wreckage the next morning. The pub was still in operation, if you wanted to clamber down the pit and scramble up to the shattered bar for your pint of mild and bitter. A sign said, "Open during altercations." A proper Britisher with bowler and furled umbrella looked at the sign with disapproval. "A bit thick, what?"

Yes, war was hell. In a war we lived day by day, because there might be no tomorrow. So the important thing was to live each day to the fullest—to keep clean, keep warm, eat well, take people for what they were. You had dreams and hopes, but not plans. Plans are for people with certain tomorrows.

But the worst part of it wasn't the danger. It was the tedium and loneliness in a foreign land. I played a lot of solitaire, also considerable poker and gin rummy with men of the office. Every day when I wasn't in the field I wrote a letter home. The Army put out instructions regarding how to write a letter home, what to say. Evidently the civilians at home got the same advice, and I received letters obviously written as a patriotic duty which were dreadfully boring and virtually impossible to reply to. Gay's letters were another thing, full of details about the home front. Gay saved my letters, but I lost all of hers. Yes, there was a war on, but she has never been able to understand my explanation of that fact.

The PRO considered that she acted under sheer inspiration when she sent the latest issue of the Montgomery Ward catalog, that incredible cornucopia of America. The book was a sensation in the office, with a waiting list. While there have been various theories as to why America became a world power, my private opinion is that Sears and Roebuck and Montgomery Ward played vital roles in it. Their catalogs amounted to sacred scriptures to us in those days. They listed every commodity available from baby chicks to two-story houses.

The only way folks in the boondocks of Zion (that meant all of us) kept aware of technological progress was through the newest mail-order catalogs. They were nearly as important to daily life as the family Bible. When buggy whips gave way to spark coils and brake linings on the catalog pages we perused, we realized that things were changing out there in the world.

Most of the things you ordered from the catalog were sent in parts and had to be assembled. Frozen-faced Buster Keaton made a comedy about trying to assemble a mail-order house. The fade out scene was of him frustrated, putting the instructions atop the mess and walking away. I subsequently wrote a story for *The Saturday Evening Post* about a budding author who ordered an unabridged dictionary and received instead one thousand baby chicks.

You waited expectantly whenever you placed an order. When the parts arrived in a sack, you might assemble them to discover that instead of the post drill you ordered, you'd received a jigsaw, or perhaps a lathe. You'd keep it, for it always was a good value, and try again.

The customer gained self-reliance assembling orders, and in turn the mail order houses relied upon him. When I got a Sears refrigerator with a crooked door, I wrote a complaint. In reply I was instructed to remove the door, place it flat on the floor, stand on it and pry up at the crooked corner until it was straight. I did, and the door worked fine.

The old catalogs were never discarded. We all knew of the customer who wrote Sears asking the price of toilet tissue. The reply came, "See page 714." He retorted, "If I had page 714, I wouldn't need toilet tissue." And what red-blooded man can forget his teenage fascination with the lovelies in the underwear section of the catalog?

The catalog represented who and what we were, the great symbol of all that we were fighting for. The catalog was America. It was home.

CHAPTER 13

THE GENERAL HAD A DATE

At Christmastime, 1944, I received one of the most precious of presents, the gift of life. I survived a B-17 bomber crash in which two men were killed. Suddenly I knew the ecstasy of the twice born.

In mid-December, I had been packing up for a field trip one evening at the PRO offices on Grosvenor Square, when the charwomen arrived. The charwomen who came to clean the offices in the evenings were a cheerful lot. Each had her own, individual accent, and the chatter that went on between them was incomprehensible. When talking to me they spoke as if they were talking to a child, slowly and distinctly. I always gave them the fruitcakes sent to me by well-meaning friends and family members back home. It was true that the fruitcakes arrived undamaged in their tin cannisters, but even while living on powdered Army chow, I couldn't choke down fruitcakes. Yet the charwomen loved them.

On this particular evening, one of the charwomen was a new girl. She was obviously fey, for as we met she exclaimed, "What a beautiful aura you have, Yank!"

"Can you see it?"

"But of course. And you were born with a cowl. You have a guardian angel watching over you. You are protected, Yank, to be sure."

I smiled and didn't really think about it again until two days before Christmas. We'd been on a field trip to a tiny oil refinery at Merkwiller, near Strasbourg, a bombing target, to assess the damage, and while there the sudden German counteroffensive in the Ardennes—the Battle of the Bulge—caught the Allies by surprise. When a Panzer unit roared past just three miles away, nobody was more surprised than the four PRO innocents wandering about the front in a jeep in dress uniform—low-cut shoes, neckties, and fifty-mission hats.

While we escaped capture, there were three hard days of driving through clammy fog to Paris. For Air Force personnel, travel by jeep was a grim hardship indeed. However, we had no choice. The German attack coincided with a pea-soup overcast that grounded every plane in Europe.

MPs stopped us at every crossroad. What state were we from? What was its capital? Who were the Brooklyn Bums? Who was the Brown Bomber? Who was FDR?—questions intended to trap Germans who parachuted behind our lines in American uniforms. While convinced we weren't spies, the MPs really didn't know *what* we were, with our natty uniforms and lack of weapons. All we carried were Colt .45 automatic pistols, which we didn't have the slightest idea how to use.

In Paris the motor pool sergeant was happy to get his jeep back. Airplanes were no problem, but jeeps were short. When our colonel had complained to headquarters that shortage of jeeps was hampering our work, the general issued an order to give the PRO all the jeeps they wanted. When we'd presented this order to the motor pool sergeant, he said, "You go tell the friggin general that I ain't *got* no friggin jeeps! So frig *him*!"

There was nothing to do in Paris; I'd worn it out. I played solitaire, saw the Follies again, caught the Grand-Guignol and a Marx Brothers movie with French subtitles. At night I slept on the floor of our office at the Scribe Hotel.

As the scheduled four-day field trip stretched into ten, I was beginning to smell and be hard to live with. My job was in London, also my laundry and letters from home. London was only an hour and twenty minutes away, except for the unending fog which kept all aircraft grounded. Tedium was driving me up the wall when I learned that a general was flying to London next day, fog or no fog. Just maybe I could hitch a ride.

The fog was just as heavy next day on the way to Villacoublay. At the airport, the officer in the control tower said perhaps the general was taking off.

"That's up to the general," he told me.

The plane was a big, gleaming B-17 bomber, the personal aircraft of General Carl A. Spaatz, Air Force Commander in Europe. Another general, named Anderson, was going to use it. This Flying Fortress was for me. I'd done a lot of flying, but always under tension, taking off and landing at bombed airfields. But this four-engine, converted bomber, lightly loaded, would be like riding in a Pullman.

A jeep came out of the fog with the pilot, copilot and navigator.

"You guys going?" the pilot wanted to know. "Okay, help turn those props over." We pushed against the props, counting twelve revolutions. General Anderson arrived, with his aide and a Royal Air Force officer; and at the sight of two stars we suddenly remembered to salute, a bit awkwardly because the PRO wasn't much on military courtesy.

Six hitchhikers followed the crew and brass inside. We were all loaded with Christmas gifts: Chanel No. 5, cognac, coffee, and champagne—all hard to find in London. By military standards, the plane was really fixed up. The interior was sheathed with plywood. The tail section held an office and kitchen, the midsection was fitted with bunks, and there were leather benches along the sides of the passenger section up front. This was traveling in style.

For the very first time, I didn't sweat out a takeoff. The paperback remained in my hip pocket. Then when we were airborne, someone said, "You can't see the wingtips." True enough, the number four engine was a vague ghost in the fog. I couldn't see the wingtip. So what? I figured. Generals don't take chances. I began reading a copy of *Yank*, the GI magazine.

After awhile, a small feeling of disquiet began gnawing at me. My watch showed we were ten minutes overdue. I still couldn't see the wingtip. Of course the general's navigator would be a pretty sharp lad, or he wouldn't have this job. But he was flying blind. There was no directional radio beam from Biggin Hill airport that could be followed in by black-painted German intruders to strafe us on the ground.

Now I was conscious of the banking and turning of the plane. Were we lost?

As the plane sank in an air pocket, my insides rose up. This is the way it had always been with me when flying, uneasy and a little sick. But it was silly this time, wasn't it?

Another ten minutes crawled by, as the plane weaved about in the fog. Where were we, anyhow?

Had it really been that important to be in London for Christmas?

About then the copilot came back and he said we were fifteen minutes out of Biggin Hill. Good. I relaxed. He went back to see the general, who returned with him to the pilot's compartment. Why? I felt sick again—and still couldn't see the wingtip.

After the general's aide went up front, we heard that a decision had to be made—whether to try a blind landing at Biggin Hill or go on to Prestwick, Scotland, where the fog wasn't so dense. Through the open door I saw the general standing between the pilot and copilot; poor devils, this fog and the general breathing on the backs of their necks.

Twenty more minutes crawled by. I kept looking at my watch, checking the second hand to see if it was running. "It's clearing up some," a passenger said hopefully. I still couldn't see the wingtip.

The aide came out and made an announcement.

"We're going in at Biggin Hill on instruments."

The plane circled and began a glide. There were no seat belts, so we braced our feet against the bench on the opposite side, with heads and shoulders shoved hard against the cushion. The engines dropped to a low throb as we glided in for the landing. Then suddenly the four engines roared again, the plane shuddering as we climbed. We'd missed the landing strip. The Fortress circled and came in again. Once more we braced for it and sweated out the landing. Once more the engines roared and we circled again for another try.

"Wish to hell I'd stayed in Paris," someone said. I realized then there were worse things than tedium.

"The general really must have a hot date in London," the GI next to me muttered. That had been our cynical explanation for this flight of the only airborne plane in Europe. It had seemed fortunate to me, the remark wryly funny. Now it was neither.

"They don't advise us to come down here," someone said. "We'll go on to Prestwick."

So I'd spend Christmas in Scotland, probably, and wouldn't be in London after all.

"Twenty-foot visibility here," someone said. I looked out again for the wingtip, but just then the engines cut again as we began gliding in. I eyed the plexiglass turret overhead, checking the position of the release handles, in case I had to get out in a hurry. Then the wheels touched down, light as a feather. Wow! What a relief! We all relaxed, blowing out our breath, grinning. Air travel was wonderful, once you were on the ground again.

At this moment we didn't know that we were headed for disaster. We didn't know that the pilot had missed the runway. It had a row of lights along either side, but with twenty-foot visibility this did him no good. He had to come in slow enough to set down. Unless he was exactly right he had to gun the engines, circle and try again, as we'd been doing for half an hour. To attempt to alter direction at slow landing speed would be suicide. On this attempt he wasn't far off the strip. The concrete was hard and smooth, the plane lightly loaded. He set her down.

What he didn't know was that he'd landed on a parking area under construction. Fortunately, we just missed a huge mound of earth and the bulldozer which had put it there. Then we began hitting the strips of concrete. The area was half paved, with alternate strips of foot-thick concrete and gaps between them.

Inside, we had just relaxed when the plane hit the first concrete strip and lurched heavily. The next strip tore off an aileron and swung us into the stack of baled straw piled there for curing the concrete. It was eerie to see straw flying past the windows. We were being shaken about, with a series of screaming bumps. The major across from me was white around the lips. The GI next to him had his mouth wide open, screaming noiselessly.

The baled straw tore off a wheel. We veered to the right, otherwise we would have crashed into the control tower. A fast series of near miracles had seen us still right side up and unhurt. Then with a tremendous crunch we hit the crash truck, mashing the GI driver between the top and the steering wheel. He was a kid of nineteen, killed instantly. The man with him sustained a broken leg.

We were still going fast, but hitting the crash truck might have saved us; it became our wheels. We rode it to a stop, while our tail made a great sweeping arc that killed a GI waiting with a fire extinguisher.

The door of the pilot's compartment sprang open. Out of it, along the ceiling, spurted deep red fire shot with strings of black smoke. The general, soaked with gasoline, scrambled out, crouched low below the fire. "Get the hell out of here!" somebody yelled. "Get your pants out of here!" We didn't need to be told.

I wasted no time, following close behind the man leading the exodus. In the compartment with the bunks was stacked the important stuff we'd brought for Christmas, but no time for it now. Back in the tail compartment a set of graniteware dishes cluttered the floor, and we tumbled about as if on roller skates. The man ahead of me slipped on the dishes and scrambled on hands and knees to the door, not taking hold of the handle but clawing at the door like a dog. I opened the door and he burst out, scurrying away on hands and knees. The gas tanks would go up any second.

I was right behind him. Then as I scrambled out, the major following me stepped aside at the door. "After you, sir," he said to the general. The major was a career officer, and never have I witnessed such a gesture of dedication to the source of all military blessings.

Fortunately, we all got out.

The first thing I saw was the poor GI who'd been wiped out by the tail. They were rolling his body carefully onto a stretcher. Firemen had saved the guy in the crash truck with the broken leg, but couldn't get the driver out. The only luck he had that day was that he didn't feel a thing when the plane hit.

There was a gigantic belch, then a huge ball of flame as the tanks went up. The aluminum shell of the plane burned like cardboard. The crash truck melted down. The water and foam they shot into the flames did nothing but throw viciously beautiful fireworks.

I reached into the fire and pulled out my smoking musette bag. I'd brought champagne and two bottles of cognac as presents, along with Chanel No. 5 perfume. Everything was broken from the heat except one fifth of cognac.

In the control tower they gave me coffee and doughnuts, which made a lead ball in my stomach. "You mean you were on that plane, Mac?" they kept asking. I felt a curious detachment, a sense of fantasy. I wasn't afraid. Not yet. I wasn't jittery. Not yet. I didn't feel that I was living on borrowed time. That was to come later. All I could feel right now was pity for the poor kids who got it on our account. It was the general's date and their lives.

The general hadn't even stayed to watch. He hadn't stopped to change his gasoline-soaked uniform, nor even borrow a hat. He'd gotten into his staff car and sped away.

The GIs griped as we rode in a recon car toward London.

"I hope the general likes that date—"

"Me, I hope she's pretty—"

"She won't get no Christmas presents from Paris, any-how—"

"Those poor bastards. They got it on his account—"

"I hope she's worth it."

It wasn't until I reached my apartment in Queen's Gardens that I began to shake. My teeth chattered. I quivered all over. Alcohol's proper use is as a medicine. The cognac was the medicine of choice. My hands trembled until it was difficult getting the cork out.

Next day, Christmas Eve, the largest bombing mission ever to leave England took off according to plan, despite the weather. Major General Frederick L. Anderson, Jr., Deputy Commander of Operations, had conferred with General Eisenhower's staff at SHAEF headquarters in France, then had to return to London to direct the dispatching of more than 2,000 heavy bombers to help stop the German counteroffensive in the Ardennes.

December 1944. Sam surveys the wreckage of the plane
crash he survived.

Yes, the general had had a date.

"You were protected, Yank," the fay charwoman told me. "You are being led, for a purpose."

I believed she was right, as I went about touching familiar things that were brand new again, seeing familiar sights with new eyes, enjoying food with new discovery, walking the streets of the old city as an explorer, greeting my friends in the office with new love and appreciation, hearing the birds sing in Hyde Park as they never had before. It was great to be alive. Everything was a Christmas gift—a second birth, a brand new world, another life. I reveled with the ecstasy of the born again.

Yes, the general's mission had been vitally important, but if we had all been killed in the crash, another officer would have taken another plane from Paris within the hour.

So I was being led toward what goal? Protected for what purpose?

At this time I had published hundreds of stories and articles in national magazines, but nothing about the Mormon culture, despite my heritage. My grandfather was LDS President John Taylor, my father Apostle John W. Taylor. My mother was a plural wife. Now I wondered if I had been spared because of my ability to write about my people for readers of the outside world, as Hugh B. Brown had urged me to do.

Hugh B. Brown was president of the British Mission, with headquarters in an old red brick building out far west on Nightingale Lane in London. When I wasn't away on a story I'd drop by of a Sunday to attend services held there for military personnel. Hugh Brown pointed out to me that our internal literature was largely intended for and

read by the LDS people. Also, most literature about
Mormons in national trade channels was critical or anti-
Mormon. With my talent as an author, he said, I could
bring understanding and appreciation for my people to an
audience who couldn't be reached by the hard sell of the
missionary approach.

The first thing I tried on President Brown's advice was an
article, "Fifty Thousand Amateur Chaplains," about the
LDS servicemen who held all the qualifications for a chap-
lain's duties without having the office. I sent this to my
New York agent, but it was too specialized for the outside
market.

However, Hugh Brown's advice made it a top priority
when I returned from the war for me to write a book about
my father's family of six wives and three dozen children. He
was kind enough to read the manuscript and make suggestions. Before publication of the book I wrote a summary of
it for *Holiday* Magazine, which the U.S. State Department
republished and distributed worldwide as Americana.
Family Kingdom was to my knowledge the first book for
the outside world which portrayed plural marriage as a way
of life, without apology or condemnation. It was published
in 1951 and is still in print.

Since then I have published nine other books about the
LDS people, and a number of magazine articles.

Yes, on that flight from Paris to London, the general had
a date. And so did I.

CHAPTER 14

THE WRITING BUSINESS

The Pentagon wanted me to stay in uniform and write the official history of the Air Force in World War II. I could have retired in seventeen and a half years as a field-grade officer on a good pension. But I'd had enough of the military, and I had other fish to fry, other books and articles to write.

I had been successfully publishing in national magazines ever since college days. In fact after dropping out of college my only nonwriting work was a period of two weeks during the early days of the war when I helped build a submarine net to save San Francisco from enemy attack. (Evidently I was the only man left in California who could read a blueprint.) My file copies of fiction stories and magazine articles I had written filled a trunk. My work ranged from short stories to serials and one-shot book-lengths. For awhile I ground out pulp paper stories: detectives, westerns, sports, adventure, even a confession. During this period I created a series character named Mullally. But it seemed that every time Mullally appeared in a magazine, it was doomed. After Mullally killed off three magazines, I killed off Mullally for the good of the writing business. It was too late, however. The pulps never did recover from Mullally.

Alas, most of the publications I wrote for are no longer in business.

One day I knocked out a routine yarn for *Detective Fiction Weekly*, but seeing how that magazine hadn't reported on a story previously submitted, I sent the new one to *Collier's*. This was like buying just one ticket in a million dollar lottery. *Colliers, The Saturday Evening Post*, and *Liberty* each received more than 5,000 unsolicited short stories a week, which were dumped in huge bins and called the "slush pile." Ponytailed office girls busily glanced at the first page and stuffed them into the return envelopes with a rejection slip.

When *Collier's* accepted "Memory Test," the event was so unusual that the girl who plucked it from the slush pile was promoted. When the check arrived—at ten times the pulp rate—I learned a basic fact of the writing business, which is that the chief difference between a high-paying and a penny-ante market is the amount of money involved. Every market requires the very best you can do. I also discovered that the better the market, the better you're treated. Nobody demands the last drop of blood like a two-bit market.

From that time on I concentrated on markets which paid the most and were easiest to write for, including *The Saturday Evening Post, Collier's, Liberty, American, Country Gentlemen, Woman's Home Companion, Esquire, True, Argosy, Blue Book, Country Home, Reader's Digest, Holiday, Family Circle*, and an extensive and nostalgic list of others.

Back in New York after my stint in the service, I found that Walt Disney hadn't forgotten me. Two of his men met me and took me to dinner. Soon after returning from the war—that was in 1945—I went down to the Disney Studio in Burbank. Walt bought the screen rights to three

Liberty stories I had published, the story of Professor Rhoade's fantastic rubber (which he called "flubber"), the miraculous pitcher of Philemon, and the flying Model T Ford. His idea was to combine the three into one motion picture. After some discussion he decided that the pitcher didn't fit in the picture. I did a tentative outline for combining the other two and went home.

Professor Rhoades would become *The Absent-Minded Professor*, which wasn't produced until 1961. But in the meantime I wasn't sitting by the phone for some fifteen years waiting for Disney to call. Walt was doing other things and so was I. In addition to writing many articles and serials, I also published eight books. *The Man with My Face* was the first thing I wrote after returning home from the war. I'd started it several times during the war, setting the story in London with the hero being an Air Force GI. But what with being in the field half the time on Air Force stories and catching up on my duties as chief of the Magazine Section of USSTAF PRO while in town, there simply wasn't sufficient time to do a book.

At home again, I set the story in Redwood City, California, and the hero lived on Stockbridge Avenue, where I do. And he had my telephone number, which, I discovered, was a mistake. The hero in the story was named Chick Graham, and when the story appeared people dialed the phone number to ask, "Is Chick there?" When it appeared in book form, again the phone rang off the hook. I portrayed Chick as a typical commuter who takes the same train to San Francisco six days a week and returns on the same afternoon train. Wednesday was just another day, except that it was the last of its kind. When he walks into his home that afternoon, his wife, his best friend, and a stranger who is his double are playing cards. His wife claims that he is an imposter, as does his best friend. The man with his face says, "Just what are you trying to get away with, mister?" They put the dog on him, and his own dog bites him. End of chapter one.

It ran as a six-part serial in *Liberty*, and the editor touted it as the best one the magazine had ever published. Before publication the editor sent the first chapter around to various confreres with the query, "Do you think Taylor can pull this off?" It had several American and eleven foreign editions (eight of them in different languages), became a book club selection and also a motion picture for which I collaborated on the screenplay.

With *The Man with My Face*, which was strictly fiction, I learned a lesson in characterization. The character of Buster, the hero's best friend, was drawn straight from life. I knew intimately a man exactly like Buster and took pride in portraying his habits, idiosyncrasies, and foibles in detail. Yet the only criticism of the manuscript by the editor of *Liberty* was "You've got to do something about Buster. He's unbelievable." Each of us is a complex individual, who plays many roles in life. In fiction, however, you simply give a man a salient characteristic and a couple of habits to fit the role he plays in this particular story. I had to simplify Buster to fit his part. *Then* he was believable.

I learned another lesson in the pains I took arranging the material for this magazine serial. I carefully arranged it so that each of the five installments would end on a high dramatic note. You can imagine my concern when the magazine ran it in six installments; yet each one still broke on a high note. I realized that if the story is interesting enough, you can cut it off almost anywhere and the reader will anxiously await the next installment.

Later, *Collier's* published my book *The Mysterious Way* as a serial. Though a comedy, it was a story of the power of faith. It was a humorous fictional piece in the setting I knew best—the Mormon culture. I was trying to follow President Hugh B. Brown's advice. The name of this first serial was changed to *Heaven Knows Why!* when it became a book and was an alternate selection of the Literary Guild. The book received excellent reviews nationally, but in Utah the roof fell in. The Saints not only didn't see the humor, but some of them didn't realize the story was fiction. One man demanded the name and address of a character who was an apostate, and every small town knew *it* was the locale I had written about. They scalped me in "Zion," saying I was making light of sacred things. But I was on to other projects and tried not to be too concerned.

Thirty years later, a friend of mine got excited about this same book, which had been out of print for ages, and decided to put it out as a paperback. At this very time, a professor at BYU wrote a piece about "Samuel W. Taylor and *Heaven Knows Why*." He said that my book was the first, last, and only funny Mormon novel he had ever seen published. We talked over the phone, and he said that now the Saints were mature enough to enjoy the humor. After chatting with this professor, Richard Cracroft, I wrote a fast preface for the paperback, praising the Saints for their mature appreciation of humor. And what do you know? After I told them it was funny, they loved it. To finish off that story, Hollywood had taken an option on *Heaven Knows Why.* Just maybe it will be the first funny Mormon motion picture ever made.

Nightfall at Nauvoo, another book I banged out while waiting for Disney to call back, is the story of the Mormon pioneer city which quickly grew to become the largest city in Illinois—twice the size of Chicago—before being abandoned as the Saints crossed the plains to Utah. Here was an epic story and I did a long book about it. It went to Macmillan. The editor phoned me to tell me he liked the book. However, the business office was afraid that with its length the cost of publication would price it out of the market. "They want you to cut 50,000 words."

Well, 50,000 words would make a respectable book in itself. But I'm a pro. "Okay, what parts don't you like?" I wanted to know.

"I like all of it. Use your own judgment."

Now, *there's* an editor I could really love. So I went at it. You don't drop 50,000 words by clipping paragraphs. I took out whole sections and brought the script down to size. And do you know what? It was a better book for it, tighter, more smoothly paced, more interesting.

Then came the matter of a title. I called it *Expel or Exterminate.* It had alliteration; it was an actual quotation by the governor of Missouri when he drove the Saints out; and the title implied the work's drama.

"It sounds like bug-killing," the editor said. "Try again."

I dreamed up twelve titles then phoned him and began reading the list. Number five was *Nightfall at Nauvoo.* He said, "That's it." So now I've got seven more good titles ahead.

Eventually, Walt called me back to finish my flying car script. My contract with Disney was fifteen pages long. Fourteen and a half pages listed what I was giving Walt, and a half page explained what Walt was giving me. But it was a fair contract, and the Disney Studio was strictly honest, which you can't say for everyone in Lotus Land. As an example of his honesty, I received royalties for years from a book, *The Flying Car,* which another man wrote and I never saw, but was based on my idea. Also, Disney had never before made a sequel, but when *Son of Flubber* was produced I had a piece of the action.

The Disney Studio was built in the form of a hospital. It had wide stairways, enormous elevators to accommodate patients being wheeled about, and a series of bays with nurses' stations and corridors leading to various wards and rooms. Why it was originally built this way I never knew, yet during my three-year stint there the place was constantly being remodeled from a hospital to a motion picture studio. It was unsettling to arrive in the morning to find your office completely bare. This didn't mean you were fired, but that the room was being remodeled and that you had another office. To accommodate this, everything in my office had a number—the typewriter, the chair, the desk, the standing lamp, the rug, the pencil sharpener, even the paper clips.

While at the studio, I learned some of what went into the Disney touch. In making the final cuts on *The Absent-Minded Professor,* Walt Disney invited various groups to the studio projection room and made changes according to audience reaction. He sat at the back alongside a man with a clipboard. Time and time again Walt would lean over and whisper something, and the man would make a note. Next showing would see changes.

For example, in one scene the Model T Ford is flying over Washington and an Air Force general says, "Shoot it out of the sky!" Another officer says, "But it might fall on Congress." The general does a take, as if this might *not* be a bad idea. The audience laughs at this, so his reply is smothered. Walt makes a note, and next time when the general does the take, he turns his head to look at the other officer, then turns back again. This gives time for the laugh to rise and fall, and we hear the next line. A small change, perhaps, but multiply it by hundreds, and it is the Disney touch.

The Absent-Minded Professor was fantasy, of course, and the basic problem with fantasy is that the audience must believe it. You had to believe that the Ford could fly. You had to believe that rubber would bounce. Otherwise, the picture would fail. The "golden arm" was the key to making the fantasy real on the screen, a gismo which cost $80,000 to make. It took the Ford off the ground, into the air, and brought the car down to earth again. It made the flying Ford convincing. The Ford on the golden arm didn't have an engine. When it came down the scene cut to a working Ford chugging away. While in the air the car, with Fred McMurray and Nancy Kelly in it, was shot against a backdrop of red velvet, which photographed neutral with black and white film. Later, by rear projection, the scenery over which the car was traveling was added. Dry ice on the floor of the soundstage made clouds. You believed that Ford was flying.

For distance shots, there was a toy Ford a yard long, with look-alike dolls in it. It was suspended from the ceiling, while men below controlled it with strings. It steered, wheels turned, lights went on and off, beep-beep. Then for greater distance there was a Ford two-feet long and another one-foot long; everything worked, beep-beep.

For the basketball game, you had to believe the rubber bounced. The bad guy team was composed of the previous year's graduates from the USC varsity team—guys six and a half feet tall, terrific players. They loved the game and kept on shooting baskets between takes. Small acrobats composed the good guys team. They *did* bounce, jumping from a platform onto a trampoline, off-camera, and sailing into the air on-camera. The final shot of the game, where a good guy sailed through the basket with the ball in his hands, was shot from an angle where you didn't see that the hoop was much larger than standard; the regular hoop wouldn't have worked.

For the cheerleaders, the union sent a group who looked like the original Floradora Sextet. Walt brought in cute college cheerleaders and paid the others union scale to keep out of sight.

In this present era when pictures can cost $30 million and up, it is rather quaint to realize that *"The Professor"* was brought in for $750,000, which included a 25% studio overhead.

I still have a Screen Writers' Annual Award in my file that says, "Nomination for Writing Achievement to Samuel W. Taylor whose *The Absent-Minded Professor* has been nominated as the best written American Comedy of 1961."

Walt was very democratic when I worked with him, and he knew everyone. "Come in at any time," he said. "My door is always open." But this was the very last thing we did, because if Walt said no, that ended it; there was no appeal. A group of men worked several years on Chanticleer, the rooster, but when Walt said no, the group moved out and started Hanna-Barbara (*The Flintstones*). A crew spent years in Australia; Walt didn't use a foot of the film. A crew spent a long time filming the salmon run; but there was no salmon with cross-eyes or big ears, no salmon with personality; one looked exactly like another. Walt whittled away at it and finally cut it to 15 minutes.

As a result, the various producers working on projects would buttonhole Walt in the hallway, the cafeteria, even in the rest room. "Walt, we're sort of thinking along these lines" they would venture, getting an informal reaction in order to avoid getting his veto later on. There were Walt experts at the studio, too—men who knew what Walt might think.

I read a book, *Disney's World,* by Leonard Mosley (Stein and Day, 1985), which portrays Walt as a frustrated and embittered martinet with "a terrible temper," who "abused and humiliated his closest friend and partner of his formative years," and was notorious for his "drunken rages." Mosley says, "Long concealed was the fact that Disney had a nervous breakdown in 1931 when he was unable to father a child and doctors hinted that the problem was not his wife's."

I knew Disney at his worst, thirty years after his so-called nervous breakdown, when he supposedly was cracking up. Yet during three stints at the studio over a period of years I never saw or heard any evidence of it. The Walt Disney I knew was a friendly, courteous, likable guy. He knew everyone in the studio on a first-name basis. In talking to other people, inside and outside the studio, I found nobody who hinted at temper tantrums or sexual hangups. There never was a whisper of a drinking problem, nor did I see any evidence of it. I batched with Rutherford Montgomery during his two-year stint at the studio, and Monty held the same high opinion of Walt that I did.

It is quite true that Walt Disney was the boss. His word was final. But he put his money where his mouth was. He backed his own judgment. And the Disney touch made his films the outstanding successes that they were. Amen.

As a footnote, let me say that the Coke machines at the Disney Studio were the only ones in Hollywood which worked for a nickel.

After my time with Disney came more books. *Uranium Fever*, or *No Talk Under One Million*; *The Kingdom or Nothing*, the biography of John Taylor (my grandfather) who was President of the Church and who represented pioneer Mormonism; and *The Rocky Mountain Empire*, which involves the transition from the pioneer to the modern culture. In addition, in collaboration with my brother Raymond, I wrote the two-volume work *The John Taylor Papers*, of particular interest to the LDS market and published in Utah.

I wrote primarily for the outside world about my people, and some Saints resent objective literature that conflicts with fond mythology. Still I have been tossed a few bouquets among the brickbats. In reprinting one of my articles in the book by William Mulder and A. Russell Mortensen, the authors said, "No talented native son knows Utah better than Samuel W. Taylor, who writes about it so gaily and so aptly." Kenneth B. Hunsaker of Utah State University, in a review of modern Mormon literature, listed *Family Kingdom* as "best Mormon biography," and *Heaven Knows Why!* as "best Mormon novel."

And before I get muscle-bound from patting myself on the back, I must admit that I've had many a strikeout also.

CHAPTER 15

THE BETTER HALF

I had been one of thousands of soldiers in London during the war. We would walk Piccadilly Circus, see the sights, go to the shows. But inevitably, we would end up sitting around the lounges at the Red Cross clubs, talking about "back home." Do you remember Joe's Hamburger back at five points? How about Coney Island on a Sunday afternoon? What would you give for a double-dip sundae at the College Malt? What's the first thing you're going to do when you get back home?

They all had their memories, but I would sit there feeling superior. They wouldn't be going back to my ever-loving Gay and the Dimicks, her family.

I used to imagine coming home from the wars with the whole family there to greet me. Gay's brothers—the doctor, the lawyer, the chemist—would be stretched out full length on my tile floor, the only comfortable position for a Dimick male. The girls and in-laws might be lying on the couch and settees, a bit on company manners after my long absence. Mom Dimick favors the footstool where she can keep her lap full of letters, a couple of hundred or so. They would all be reading letters and passing a dollar bill.

Whenever the Dimick clan gathers, they all bring out their accumulated letters and dump them into Mom's lap.

She hands them out and they go around the circle. It doesn't matter who they're from or what they're about, or how old they are. The Dimicks like to read letters: love letters, business letters, bills, anything that comes in an envelope. No wonder Gay was able to produce every one of my letters after the war.

It is for this reason that I kept my letters home breezy, newsy, and somewhat restrained. I never have developed the true Dimick spirit when it comes to sharing personal correspondence. When I was pursuing Gay, I courted her for a year or so by mail while she was living in California. After I scratched up enough money for a visit, I arrived to find Gay's sister Nell and brother Keene (who were living with Gay and attending San Jose State College at the time) busily working math problems on the back of a couple of letters I had written behind closed doors. Another time, I wrote a love letter to Gay, who shared it with Nell, who sent it off to Bill, who was in the Marines at the time. My letter ended up posted on the bulletin board of a battleship as a model, and I understand several thousand GI sweethearts received missives full of flowery allusions and tender sentiments shortly thereafter.

The dollar-bill game is a little more difficult to explain. After all my years in the family, I still haven't quite mastered the rules. Maybe you have to be potential multi-millionaires like Gay's brothers. The game goes like this. In the midst of the talk and hubbub, Max will produce a dollar bill and hand it to Georgia, saying, "Here, I owe you this, remember?"

Georgia is thunderstruck. She denies any knowledge of the debt and accuses Max of a plot to force something on her. A violent argument ensue, with the entire family chipping in. Reluctantly, Georgia finally accepts the bill. She immediately turns to Dan, and the scene is repeated. The Bill goes on to Gay, to Mom, to Nell, to Elise, to Keene, and back to Max again. The game occupies the better part of an evening and seems to be fun for all.

The Dimicks' sharing of letters and passing the dollar bill might be simply another manifestation of the Dimick urge to give something to someone. This urge exceeds all bounds. You have to be extremely careful what you say around the Dimicks. They're sensitive. If you mention anything from a living room suite to a sailboat, a truck might arrive with it in a couple of days.

The Dimicks have even been known to share children, and when I got home from the war, my writing career and Disney weren't the only things waiting for me. I found two little girls had joined Gay and I in our house in Redwood City.

Sara, born in the spring of 1944, was the child of Gay's sister Elise. Elise had to be off to Oregon, to join her husband, Arthur, who was in the Army there, and Gay began caring for Sara the day she came home from the hospital. I maintain that Gay's sister Georgia then felt that we should have two children instead of one, and so she manufactured Elizabeth especially for us. Elizabeth was Georgia's third child in three years. This on top of war hysteria proved to be too much for Georgia at the time, and Gay stepped in to help her. Sara was two and Elizabeth was one when I was mustered out of the Army. Elizabeth was our charming visitor for seven years, and then continued to come and go around our home for the rest of her life. Gay and I adopted Sara.

Coming back home to Gay was the best thing I could do for my writing career. It takes a certain kind of woman to put up with the writing life, which of course included having no wage-paying job. Back before Xerox, Gay copied on the typewriter the 325 pages of Cecil A. Snider's M.A. thesis, "Development of Attitudes in Sectarian Conflict: A Study of Mormonism in Contemporary Newspaper Sources." This thesis was invaluable to my research for *Nightfall at Nauvoo*. Gay is always the first to read any manuscript. If a section bothers her, I might not agree with her suggestions for a rewrite, but I know something needs work, and I revise it.

As a writer, I have always found Gay to be my best friend and severest critic. Under questioning, she might say the same for me. According to her, the first thing I said upon discovering her identity was, "Did you write the prize Christmas story published in the *Y News* last year? Let me tell you what was wrong with it." Gay maintains that I am an incurable critic. I did relent once. Upon our first sight of the Golden Gate Bridge, I commented that I would have thought the engineers would have done things differently. A minute later, however, I said I supposed that the engineers knew what they were doing. Gay claims that she almost fell out of the car in astonishment and that with this pronouncement, I added a certain unease to our marriage. She says she never knows when I might approve of something again.

My persuading Gay to marry me in only five years was something of an achievement. No Dimick is hasty in marriage. Georgia and Oscar's romance went on for six or seven years. Dan decided after some seven years that he knew

Dorothy well enough. He was in New York with the Justice Department and she was in Utah. She hadn't heard from him in several months when a telegram arrived saying that if she felt like getting married, she should come to New York and they'd visit The Little Church around the Corner.

Bill and Nell take the cake, though. Bill kept after Nell from the time they were kids together in Nampa. The pursuit got hectic for about seven years before Nell finally said yes, and Bill no doubt sighed with great relief. But not for long. They immediately climbed onto a bus for Detroit to buy a new car and drive it home. For three nights Bill sat holding hands on the bus with his bride. When they got to Detroit, the salesman made them a proposition. Why not drive two cars home, sell one, and pay the expenses of the trip?

This wasn't particularly Bill's idea of a honeymoon, but Nell has the business head of the family.

"I think it's a wonderful idea," she said. What she didn't mention was that she didn't know how to drive a car.

So they got two cars and started out. Nell put her car into low gear and got it into motion. She knew that much. She figured she'd pick up the rest as she went along. As she rounded the corner from the salesroom, she spotted a nice young fellow standing there with his thumb out. So she stopped and asked him if he could drive a car. Sure, he could drive a car. How far was he going? He was going to California.

"Hop in," Nell said.

They lost Bill in the Detroit traffic at the first stoplight.

Bill didn't catch up until they got to Utah. Nell never has understood why Bill didn't like Freddie. The Dimicks are friendly people. Freddie was a nice boy and he could drive a car. That was all.

Gay and I made one memorable bus trip of our own during our marriage. After the Los Angeles Temple was dedicated in 1956, the temple excursion from the San Francisco Bay area became much more convenient than the old trip to Utah. By this time my ever-loving wife and I were turning gray, but by the same token, we'd been married long enough to want it to last, so we joined an excursion from Redwood City to Los Angeles.

On an unforgettable Friday night, we boarded a chartered bus. Being polite, I didn't join the rush for seats and ended up alone on the wide rear seat, which was upholstered with plastic slick as ice. Besides that, the bus had square wheels, a leak in the exhaust system, and, I suspected, no springs. As noxious fumes filled the air, I slid back and forth as the bus lurched around curves. After a couple of hours of torture, the passengers began screaming. I almost joined in before I realized that they were singing.

We arrived at the temple with two hours to spare before it opened. Ah, the blessed relief. Now I had the entire rear seat to stretch out on and sleep.

"All out!" bawled the heartless driver. So we lined up at the temple door in the thin chill of the morning smog, waiting, while our arches sagged and veins swelled. Finally, the doors opened.

"This line for the living," a lady said. "This line for the dead."

"Which one," Gay muttered, "for the half dead."

The ceremony turned out to be every bit as spiritually fulfilling as others had said it would be. Yet I must admit that facing the prospect of the return trip, I felt like the condemned man eating a hearty last breakfast. It wasn't until I put the trip into the perspective of my pioneer ancestors that it's true value came to light. The trip was of enormous value, something to be treasured, not despite the hardships, but because of them. You paid a stiff price for the experience, but the higher the price, the more valuable the rewards.

Gay has always had a good sense for the true value of things. After Sara, our daughter, married Paul Weston, they lived in San Jose for a number of years, where she pursued her career as a high school Spanish teacher. Gay wanted her closer, so she persuaded me to offer them a free lot on our Redwood City property. This was high-priced real estate. I had rejected an offer of two-million dollars for my acre of backyard.

"But what would we do with the money?" Gay said. "We don't need it, and you know what they do when they sub-divide. First they cut down the trees. Then they dig a trench down the driveway for utilities. After that you have the trucks coming and power saws screaming, hammers pound-ing, workmen yelling—you wouldn't be able to write a word for I don't know how long. And the developers want to sub-divide it into eight lots. Do we want eight families in the backyard?"

I saw her point. But I couldn't help but wonder what I would have done if I'd taken the two million. I figured I'd buy a Rolls Royce and hire a chauffeur to take me around to the garage sales.

We gave Sara and Paul the lot, and that gift has been the best investment we ever made. As Gay and I have made our way into the twilight years, Sara has become our wheels, running errands and doing the shopping. Our beautiful daughter has become my secretary, medicine dispenser, my right hand in every way. And Gay has passed on to her her own secrets in the art of bread-making. Making bread like Gay does, like writing a novel, is an art, not a science. Paul has taken over as family handyman. He mows the tall grass in the acre behind the house to keep the fire danger down, tends to some rental units we own and other heavy jobs. When I travel to writers conferences, either he or Sara comes along to smash baggage, drive the rental car, smooth the way.

So Gay and I leave maintenance to the kids while we go about our routine, such as reading the morning paper. We do this at breakfast, rarely looking up. In fact for years, I parted my hair in the middle. Then I decided to comb it straight back. A couple of years after the change, Gay looked up from the breakfast paper and said, "When did you quit parting your hair?"

Though we don't share my polygamist background, Gay comes from similar, solid stock. She was born at her grandmother's home in Soda Springs, Idaho, and delivered by a midwife. Her father, Ephraim John Dimick, known as E. J., owned a herd of sheep and was his own sheepherder, so baby Gay spent the first four years of her life in a canvass-topped sheep wagon, together with her parents and sister Georgia. They had a table on hinges which was lowered for meals, and the bed stretched crosswise at the back of the wagon.

Gay's mother had been a school teacher, and she taught Gay at home until the second grade. It was a two-mile trip by horseback for Gay the next year, riding behind Georgia. Winters were severe, so mother taught the children at home for the three coldest months. Over time, transportation improved to buggy and sleigh.

E. J., Gay's father, had something of a short fuse. The family eventually homesteaded in Bancroft, Idaho, and in 1912, more water was needed for the growing town. The water company, invoking the law of eminent domain, dug three wells in the canyon and surveyed the route for a pipeline. The survey placed the pipe right through the edge of E. J.'s garden, which would uproot the yellow roses along his fence and a hedge of sweatpeas and hollyhock.

E. J. was proud of his flower garden, and as the digging crew approached, he said, "It appears to me that you fellers are thinking of putting that pipe through my garden. If so, you can think again. You can put it ten feet further south along the edge of the road."

"The survey says we can put it through the garden."

E. J. went into the house and reappeared with his .30-.30 rifle.

"The survey might say you can, but this rifle says you can't."

The pipeline went outside the garden.

When Gay was thirteen, the family moved to Nampa, where Gay attended eighth grade and high school before heading off to Brigham Young University. The rest, as they say, is history.

Sam at work

CHAPTER 16

THE PRINCIPLE PROBLEM: THE BOOK STOPS HERE

For a period of thirteen years I interviewed my mother regarding her life story.

"But, Samuel, we've talked about this before, many times."

"Okay, let's try it again."

Her dearest wish was that I should write "The Biography," the story of my father's great family of six wives and three dozen kids. The gathering of materials was, to her, akin to the search for the Holy Grail. She accompanied me on research trips to Mexico and Canada. She introduced me to confreres of John W. Taylor in business enterprises and Church affairs. Yet it seemed impossible to break through the mother-son relationship in order to interview her in depth about her life with Father. She could have said things to a stranger on a bus which she didn't seem able to tell me as her child.

Among the other five branches of the family, the reaction to the project ranged from lukewarm to active opposition. Aunt Ellen, the youngest wife, had died. Aunt May, the first wife, and the only legal Mrs. John W. Taylor, remained aloof. Wife number two, Aunt Nellie, had for years considered herself official family biographer and keeper of the archives; I was stepping on her toes. The Welling sisters,

Aunt Roxie and Aunt Rhoda, were cooperative but sensitive
about coming into the family after the Manifesto, which led
to my father's fall from grace. And the general consensus
was that I was too "negative" and unspiritual to write the
typical "family" book. This was completely true. I had no
intention of doing a family mug job. I wanted an honest
book.

Objectively, as an author standing apart, I saw my father
as a rare type of individual unique to the Mormon culture.
He was at once a high Church official and also a big-time
promoter—colonizing, constructing dams and irrigation
projects of the type now done by the U.S. Government. He
dealt in timber and coal properties ("Large tracts only,"
according to his letterhead) and had a gold mine in Mexico.
Yet in Church work he was a most successful missionary.
An inspiring speaker, Apostle Taylor was known as the
prophet of the Quorum. His wives were spirited beauties,
dedicating their lives to a lost cause which was never supposed to be easy, but was, on the contrary, to be a furnace
to burn the dross from the gold.

Mother and I believed that the story of family life in
plural marriage had never been honestly or accurately told.
Nothing was more misunderstood in the outside world,
while even among the Saints themselves, the Principle was
something past, forgotten, hush-hush, no longer to be
mentioned. Inasmuch as I was one of the very last to have
grown up in it, who would tell this story if I didn't?

I couldn't deny the widespread interest in my involve-
ment in polygamy. I don't know how many times I've
been buttonholed in the hallway at a Church function or
phoned long distance by someone who was compelled to

discuss his/her most vital subject, the Principle. But they never wanted it known that they had talked to me.

Their secret is safe with me. I can never remember a name, and I invariably forget a face. One time I entered the polls on election day and one of the officials said, "Sam Taylor! Fancy meeting you here!"

"So good to see you again." I was boggled. She was a pretty woman, but I didn't have the foggiest idea why I should know her. "Let's see, where were we the last time?"

"Always kidding!" she laughed. "I sat next to you at the California Writers Club dinner last night."

That kind of a memory made it imperative for me to write everything down as I continued through the years doing research on my father's life. And the more research I did, the more I knew I had to write *Family Kingdom*. So I rushed in where angels feared to tread.

Inasmuch as my father had died when I was eight years old, everything pertaining to his life, aside from my early memories, had to come from other sources. And the fact that he'd been excommunicated meant that most sources of information were closed. You can be sure that there was no whooping and hollering and dancing in the streets when I arrived in Salt Lake City to begin research on a former member of the Quorum of the Twelve who had been cut off for taking wives after the Manifesto.

Aunt Nellie was working at the Salt Lake Temple at the time I began my research. She knew her way about and personally introduced me at the Church Historian's Office. Without this, I don't know what materials I might have obtained from this great repository; but with it, I was shown one 3 x 5 card saying that John W. Taylor had been excommunicated. And this, I was told, was all the information available.

As I interviewed his former friends and associates, the freeze definitely was on. On the phone one man said, "Did I know John W. Taylor!—I used to sign his name for him!" But next day when I interviewed the man, he had forgotten it all.

Two of my father's brothers, Fred and Frank Y., advised me to drop the project. I could understand Uncle Frank's position—long time president of Granite Stake, and a latter-day polygamist, quietly accepted. Uncle Fred, however, had been outraged by the treatment accorded his brother by men equally guilty, and he protested by taking off his garments. To remove the sacred underclothing was, in Utah, comparable to burning the U.S. flag.

We were very close to Uncle Fred. He was the family doctor and, as previously mentioned, never presented a bill. He was a prominent physician, a founder of Provo General Hospital and active in civic affairs. Yet while he never put his garments back on, and in fact was buried in a business suit rather than his temple robes, he didn't want John W.'s story told, for fear it would injure the wives. "These noble women have had enough trouble, Sam," he told me.

The situation was delicate. While my father had been excommunicated, his wives remained in good standing in the Church. Nellie worked at the Salt Lake Temple, Ellen at the Church-owned Beneficial Life Insurance Co., Roxie and Rhoda at the Primary Children's Hospital. Then there was the check for thirty-five dollars which still arrived for my mother each month from Salt Lake.

In interviewing latter-day polygamists, many of them

from Mexico, where plural marriages were performed many years after the Manifesto, I found them passionate in their defense of the Principle. It was common for them to break down in tears at the prospect of abandoning a plural wife and her children. But write about it? Definitely not. Many of them had moved to Provo, where they lived quietly with their families, unmolested. Let sleeping dogs lie. And of course the "old maids"—the secret plural wives living alone and without children, whom my mother knew—would be shattered by exposure.

Over a period of years, I wrote letters by the hundreds. But even after my research took me to Mexico and Canada, I did not have enough information for a book. Almost my only supporters, it seemed, were other outcasts. Joseph W. Musser, leader of the largest Fundamentalist group, had recently started a monthly periodical, *Truth*, which for a period of twenty years was to hammer away at the secret and suppressed history of the Principle, both in pioneer days and during the "grand conspiracy" following the Manifesto, with which my father was involved. He had collected stories about John W. Taylor and devoted most of one issue to him. Musser mailed a copy of *Truth* to my home each month. I found thirty issues awaiting me when I returned from overseas after World War II. This file was invaluable in documenting the secret story of latter-day polygamy.

Aunt Ellen, the last and youngest wife and the first to join John in the hereafter, had a daughter named Juana who did surprise me with letters written to her mother, one a touching welcome by my mother to the new bride entering the established family. The Welling sisters, Aunts Roxie and Rhoda, told me of their courtships and marriages, and of their life in the Mexican colonies where, typically, my father had "remodeled" a modest home into a mansion for them.

On several occasions I tried and failed to interview Aunt Nellie in depth. She was the public wife during good times, the Canadian wife when the family went underground. It was at Nellie's home in Salt Lake that my father died. But beyond these facts I couldn't penetrate, whether interviewing her alone or with my mother present. Though she tried to be cooperative, she seemed on stage, giving a performance. It was an excellent performance, for she was a superb actress; but it wasn't an in-depth interview.

I had been doing research for about ten years when Aunt Nellie agreed to give me access to the materials she had accumulated regarding her husband's life. I was most grateful for this. She had made the offer, I believe, because she realized that time was running out for her, and she did want the biography written.

I headed to Salt Lake, where I found that she had about a half bushel of deeds, contracts, business correspondence, and personal letters, a veritable gold mine. For two weeks I sorted through the material, selecting pertinent papers, and ended up late one night with a package about six inches thick, which I addressed to myself in California and intended to take to the express office next day. When I arrived at the house next morning, there was a note atop the package from Aunt Nellie, which said, "The spirit of my departed brother, Douglas, appeared to me in the night with a message. He warned me, 'Don't let Sam have that material.'"

Well, this was straight from the spirit world, where I had no clout, so I left the package on the table and grabbed a train back to California. Soon Roxie and Rhoda requested that I return to them my notes on their interviews, which I did (though retaining a carbon). For three more years I kept interviewing my mother, but couldn't break through the wall. After thirteen years of effort, I still had no book.

It was my brother Raymond who suggested that in order to break through the barrier, I should take Mother to California, away from the family, away from her rose bushes, her Relief Society and Daughters of Utah Pioneers activities. She was a busy person, with a hundred reasons why she couldn't possibly leave home. It was only after Raymond said bluntly, "Do you want the biography written, or don't you?" that she agreed to come.

En route, we stopped at Grantsville in the afternoon. On the outskirts of town stood the tall Lombardy poplars she remembered as a child at the ranch where she was born. A corner of her mother's stone house remained standing. Nothing was left of the adobe home of her father's first wife, Maria, except the outline of the foundation. Maria's house, she recalled, was a way station along the underground, where pregnant plural wives stayed upstairs while en route to have their babies outside of Utah. In the willows near the creek was the frame house of the third wife, Polly. We found a hobo asleep on the floor and didn't disturb him.

Mother reminisced as we drove on. I listened. Then at Redwood City the next morning we went out back to my office. I sat at the typewriter. She sat behind me on the couch. She began talking about her life, a free association of ideas, one drifting into another, while I typed furiously. At last I'd broken through.

"Samuel, I don't know how you'll ever make sense of things," she said, "me jumping about."

"Don't worry about that. Keep talking."

We'd started that morning at 8:30, and by 10:00 that night I was bushed.

"Mother, you look awfully tired," I suggested.

"Oh, I'm not at all weary. Let's keep on another couple of hours, Samuel."

After ten days of this I was wobbling. But I had my book. It took me another year to do the final writing.

Mother's health wasn't too good after that. At eighty she thought nothing of climbing onto the steep roof to shovel off the snow, but at eighty-five she couldn't do it any more, and it exasperated her to be limited. "I think I strained myself," she admitted. "Doctors tell us to slow down after sixty. But I didn't begin to slow down until after eighty." Her library contained just about every book in print on how to stay young, and she took great pride in keeping sharp, alert, and independent. When the infirmities of age began to overwhelm her, she resisted to the bitter end. She went down swinging.

"If you go to bed at my age, you stay there," she declared when doctors tried to get her to conserve her strength.

Lillian and Ruth took turns trying to be with her and getting her to eat proteins instead of health foods. But Mother wasn't going to be tended like an invalid, and after a proper visit she'd kick the nurses out—"Lillian, now you go home. Your family needs you, and I don't." Lillian would go, and Mother would stock the refrigerator with whey and alfalfa sprouts again.

"I have every speck of ambition I ever had," she told me the last time I saw her. "I get up in the morning with the day all planned, things I want to do—and then I wilt in a couple of hours. It makes me so mad!"

As her physical strength dwindled, she came to feel that she had been here long enough. If she was going to be useless here, better to start fresh in the hereafter. Her work was done here, and there was so much to be accomplished throughout eternity with John.

One day an old friend who had taken sick sent word that he wished to see her. She planned to see him the following week, but in the meanwhile he died. "What a shame that Carl passed on before I saw him," she said. "He knew he was going, and he wanted to take a message from me to John. Carl knew that when he got to the other side, John would ask him, 'and how is Nettie?' And now Carl will have to tell him, 'Well, John, I haven't seen her lately.'"

Such was the complete and simple faith my mother had.

My thoughts were never far from the book my mother wanted so much to see finished. With her failing health, it was a good thing I was able to get her to talk when I did. She saw the book in manuscript form, and as I read it to her she corrected any errors. She also filled me in with details she hadn't mentioned previously. She was very happy about the book; it was a dream come true.

Raymond got Hugh B. Brown to read the manuscript of *Family Kingdom*. At the time he read the manuscript, he was on the faculty of BYU. Later, as first counselor in the Church presidency, he administered Church affairs during the period when President David O. McKay's vitality was at a low ebb. I had a very high opinion of Brown, and was happy that he liked the book. Raymond also got a Church committee to read the manuscript. He phoned me in Hollywood, while my play *The Square Needle* was in rehearsal, and spent an hour listing every niggling objection and suggested correction. I made the changes *and* I found an interested publisher.

Editors generally get creative when it comes to titles. I had long called my book *Family Kingdom*. The editor had a better idea: *Papa Was a Polygamist*. It had alliteration and zonk, he said. And it was commercial. *Family Kingdom* wouldn't sell books. Well, I'd spent thirteen years on that book, and I wasn't going to see it with a cheap title. Now, a writer isn't supposed to veto suggestions by an editor, but this writer did. It was *Family Kingdom* or send the manuscript back. But I've since wondered how many sales were lost because of the title.

The Square Needle was running at the Las Palmas Theater when galleys for the book arrived. I took them out east of Los Angeles, to share with my sister Rhea (May's daughter) who was running a home theater for handicapped children. I'd never met Rhea, and wanted to be able to say I knew the entire family. With her own hands Rhea had ripped out the interior of her house, except for the kitchen, and made it into a theater. I found her tough, opinionated, and hardheaded—just like me. After a violent argument we ended up friends. I'd brought along a photographer, who wanted pictures of me and Rhea reading the galleys in company with her race horse. The brute had a vicious reputation. It took two grooms to handle him at the track.

"Hold him short," Rhea said, handing me the halter rope. "If you give him slack he'll strike you." Whereupon she brushed the beast off with a broom, crawling under his belly in the process. "Oh, he won't hurt me," she said. "He knows I love him." Somehow we finished reading the galleys and I got them back to my publisher.

I had started my research in 1935. After treading a thorny path that no one would believe without having followed it, *Family Kingdom* was published in 1951. Even though there was a hiatus of two and a half years while I was fighting World War II with my typewriter and couldn't work on the book, it was a long road.

When I published a synopsis of the book in *Holiday* magazine, the U.S. State Department asked permission to circulate the article worldwide as Americana. I was most happy to give it. At last the gentile world would have a chance to understand the Principle.

However, the article conflicted with official mythology in several instances, one being the fact that at the time of my parents' marriage the ceremony could be performed, with full authority, outside the temples. John W. Taylor and Janet Maria Woolley were united for time and all eternity during a carriage ride in Liberty Park at Salt Lake.

"Lies! Lies! Lies!" thundered a prominent Church official when the book was released, citing the account of the marriage in particular. Well, I doubt if my mother would have been mistaken about it.

The other branches of our family were unhappy about the *Holiday* piece. They objected to John W. Taylor being portrayed as a man with a sense of humor, as one prone at times to take hunches as inspiration, as deeply spiritual but with Word of Wisdom "habits." He did love his coffee. And, I'm afraid, so did many in his family. It took a long time for the Word of Wisdom to become enthroned in Mormondom. In the early days, it was talked about a lot, but minor infractions were easily forgiven.

For example, my father was at our summer cabin in Provo canyon with Aunt Nellie's family when several Church brethren unexpectedly dropped in and, of course, stayed for dinner. There was nothing in the cabin to drink except coffee, so Aunt Nellie served it, apologizing for the fact that these substitutes just didn't have the flavor. But it wasn't bad, the guests agreed, holding out cups for a refill.

During the period of researching and writing the book, I had been strictly an "eating" Mormon. When a badly mimeographed postcard arrived announcing a ward dinner, I would attend because the food was good and the price was right. At the dinner a stranger might introduce himself as the new bishop; thus I kept abreast of things. I remained inactive until three years after *Family Kingdom* was published in 1951, because I was certain there would be concern at Church headquarters over a book concerning an apostle who had been unchurched for taking latter-day wives. If it were to happen to me, I didn't want to have far to fall.

When it didn't happen, and I walked into Redwood City Ward chapel, I asked, "Where do the gray-haired, hump-backed, and beat-up deacons go?" I wasn't there because I was born again, but because I was breathing again. Every Mormon author of a "New York" book about his people holds his breath, for many LDS authors have been subject to Church discipline because of the content of their books.

The original disapproval of Maurine Whipple's Mormon novel, *The Giant Joshua*, literally shattered her and her career as an author. She intended it to be the first book of a trilogy, but never wrote the other two. After almost a half century, BYU scholars have judged it as the "best Mormon novel" to date. I corresponded with Maurine, but never met her.

LaMar Petersen was called to a Church court for writing *Hearts Made Glad*, a well-documented account of the drinking habits of the sainted pioneers . . . and the list goes on. With the silencing of much of our best creative talent, it is little wonder that the literature of the managed press within the Zion Curtain is primarily propaganda, designed not to inform but to convince and convert. Preston Nibley wrote a biography of Brigham Young without mentioning that he had plural wives. *The Words of Joseph Smith*, by Andrew F. Ehat and Lyndon W. Cook, praised for its accuracy, doesn't mention polygamy.

The Achilles heel of a managed press is that it can condemn, censor, and silence, but it cannot foster good literature. It can produce little except propaganda, which is without credibility outside its borders. When Russia was a dictatorship, only the underground *samizdat* had credibility beyond the Iron Curtain. In Deseret, much the same situation exists within the Zion Curtain.

It generally takes about ten years for a "New York" book to penetrate the Zion Curtain and become "acceptable." As time passed, *Family Kingdom* became recognized as something of a minor classic. *Family Kingdom* has been used in Church history classes at BYU because it is the only candid account of the Principle as a way of life. However, in the university library the book is listed under "fiction." This means there was never such a person as John W. Taylor nor his six wives and thirty-six children. That would also mean there is no such person as Samuel W. Taylor, the author!

In 1974, Sam Weller, the big independent book dealer in Salt Lake, republished *Family Kingdom*. For the new edition I supplied three anecdotes unknown when writing the original. One was about John W. Taylor receiving five thousand dollars three days before Christmas and giving it all away until on Christmas Eve he had to borrow a nickel carfare. This explained why he died broke (not poor, broke; he never was poor).

Another story was of his funeral, the only occasion when all six wives met together, and how at the close of the service the family bade good-bye to a great soul in a gale of laughter. In view of the frank and iconoclastic character of John W. Taylor, the empty form of this ceremony was everything he hadn't wanted. Nothing could be said about this world or the next that remotely referred to the real John W. Taylor because of his excommunication. At last, thankfully, came the closing prayer—more platitudes, more meaningless bromides. The good brother offering it was sincere enough, but laboring under the handicap of being required to utter words devoid of all meaning and spirit. Also, his dental plates were loose. Each phrase began and ended with a small whistle. To the family the undulating whistle, punctuating a meaningless assortment of clichés, made it seem as if the entire ceremony were being burlesqued in gibberish.

A restlessness swept over the family. My mother bit her lip for self-control. The kids began to quiver, and then my brother Raymond was the first to break. Even knowing that it was the worst possible thing to do, he burst into wild laughter. The laughter ran through the smaller kids and then burst from the lips of the older ones. Even the six widows broke. They, of course, quickly controlled themselves, burying their faces in their handkerchiefs while shaking with the tearing and bitter mirth that was their only possible reaction to the travesty. I like to think that John W. Taylor, who fought all his life against sham and pretension, enjoyed the laughter at his funeral. It was the best farewell his family could give him at the time.

The third account was of the reinstatement of John W. Taylor to his former membership, priesthood, and blessings—almost a half-century after his death. In his last days on earth he had told my mother not to worry about the action which had resulted in his official excommunication from the Church in which he had been a member of the Twelve.

"Things will be straightened out on the other side, Nettie," he told her.

We liked to think that this was so, but as years and decades passed, things weren't straightened out on *this* side. He was still officially consigned to the buffetings of Satan. It was the dearest wish of Mother that he should be reinstated. But she had gone to join him by the time official action was finally taken.

In 1925, nine years after my father's death, Raymond began efforts to have our father, John W. Taylor, reinstated to his former station in the Church. Raymond's early attempts received the sort of encouragement given to a patient with terminal illness—there is always hope. He kept at it year after year, however. I didn't think it mattered, particularly since my father hadn't seemed to worry about it.

Forty years after he began the process, Raymond urged me to use my influence in the matter, because of my acquaintance with Hugh B. Brown. I was working in Hollywood in 1965 when Raymond phoned, insisting that *now* was the time. Since his efforts had met with forty years of failure, I wasn't too keen on the project. However, I dropped a note to Hugh Brown, now in the First Presidency, asking him what steps needed to be taken. A while later, I was working at the Brigham Young University Motion Picture Department when Hugh Brown phoned, saying that he'd discussed matters with Church President David O. McKay, who wanted to talk with me about it. I suggested that he talk with Raymond, who had worked forty years on the case and whose Church position was superior to mine.

"President McKay wants to talk with *you*."

I was without transportation, so I borrowed the studio loaner—the Brown Bomber, an ancient Chevy with bald tires and no spare. I took my daughter, Sara, and her friend along, both BYU students, for the drive to Salt Lake, where I talked with Elder Brown. He advised me to state the case briefly because of the fragile health of President McKay.

I met with the First Presidency at President McKay's office on the eighth floor of the Hotel Utah. The meeting lasted less than five minutes. Elder Tanner of the First Presidency moved that my petition be granted. President McKay agreed and he told me to write a letter for presentation to the Quorum of the Twelve for their confirmation.

Composing such a letter wasn't the easiest assignment in the world, so I took the girls across the street to the drug store and brooded while nursing a Coke. Then back to Elder Brown's anteroom, where I borrowed a typewriter from his secretary and wrote the letter.

The official verdict was that "if the Lord should judge Brother Taylor in being justified in the last three marriages he can then adjust it in the realms beyond the grave," which was exactly in accord with my father's sentiments.

In May 1965, Raymond stood proxy for Father while the necessary ordinances were performed. John W. Taylor was officially reinstated to Church membership, with his priesthood and blessings restored.

It was remarkable what the reinstatement did for my father's image. He was not only "rescued from Satan's buffetings" but from the whipping boy role of an apostate. Whereas previously nothing good could be said about him publicly, now even establishment people could find praiseworthy things about his memory. Suddenly it was okay to remember good things about my father, to talk freely about him, praise his vision and initiative, chuckle at his warmth of spirit, honor his fearless plunges into ventures of dam building and irrigation projects. What a man! The difference was as night to day. At last I understood why Raymond had wanted the official action. John W. Taylor had at last resumed his rightful place as prophet of the Quorum.

Among historians who haven't heard of the reinstatement, there is still the casual defamation of character. In the *Utah Historical Quarterly,* Winter 1979, Merrill Singer contributed a piece, "Nathaniel Baldwin, Utah Inventor and Patron of the Fundamentalist Movement," in which he lists John W. Taylor among a Fundamentalist group of 1922. My father died in 1916. And I wrote a letter to Ben Bradlee and Dale Van Atta, protesting a statement in their book *Prophet of Blood: The Untold Story of Ervil LeBaron and the Lambs of God.* In it they state that in 1923 Ervil's father "at the urging of excommunicated Apostle John W. Taylor, took a second wife." At this time my father had been dead seven years.

Though my father was reinstated in 1965, it was not acknowledged in the *Church Almanac* for many years. I wrote to the publisher several times, trying to correct the omission: no answer, no correction. Finally, twenty-eight years later, two friends with clout joined the crusade, and John W. Taylor was officially out of Satan's clutches.

As for the family itself, some of them didn't appreciate *Family Kingdom* as much as others. Some branches called my book "Nettie's story." They await the *real* biography of John W. Taylor based on Aunt Nellie's material. She passed on, and the mantle fell upon her daughter, Florence. Florence died without finishing the project. Her husband, Clyde Miller, became biographer. I heard rumors, time and again, that the book was nearing completion. After Clyde died, his sons kept on. And now, I hear, after some forty years, the book is finished at last. I wish it well. Certainly John W. Taylor deserves more than one biography, particularly one more containing Aunt Nellie's material. However, I still feel that in *Family Kingdom* I did present the truth of our family's way of life as accurately as I could.

The problem of presenting essential truth was neatly stated by columnist George F. Will. In a piece about BYU he defined Utah as an enclave surrounded on all four sides by reality. To this I will add two things. First, after having written nine books and considerable magazine material about my people, I can assure you that it is with good reason the Mormon people call themselves a "Peculiar People." Second, when I became active in the Church again, I made the remarkable discovery that the Wasatch Front wasn't confined to Utah. It wasn't a matter of geography, but of people. The Redwood City California Ward was exactly like the Fourth Ward of Provo. The Peculiar People in it were as interchangeable as Ford parts. A member could move from Provo to Redwood City on Monday, be visited by the bishop, assigned a job, and be a functioning part of the intricate mechanism by the following Sunday. And, I realized, like it or lump it, I was one of the Peculiar People, home again.

THE STRANGER IN THE MIRROR

It happened overnight. I went to bed feeling great and woke up next morning sick as a dog. And I was getting stiff. What had happened? Poison? I didn't know. Neither did the doctors. But it was serious enough. My brother-in-law is a doctor and he told me later that his prognosis was that I had no more than six months to live. As the illness deepened, the face I shaved in the mirror looked a little less like mine each day. The greatest change was in the eyes: the full-lidded and rather prominent eyes I had inherited from my maternal grandfather, Samuel Woolley, gave way to the sunken and tight-lidded ones so characteristic of my other grandfather, John Taylor.

Two of my brothers had died, and I had noted that, in the casket, each had lost his individuality to his heritage and had looked not like himself but remarkably like John Taylor. Now it was happening to me.

At the clinic, the doctors were making many tests, searching for the enemy. Perhaps an unknown virus, perhaps a poison, or perhaps—a shrug, "We don't know." I understood: perhaps an unlocated malignancy.

As day by day my body prepared to return from whence it came, I wondered, *who was this being, this physical entity, with whom I had lived all of my life?* It depended upon me, and I depended upon it, in a most intimate relationship. Yet how very little I knew about it. And now that the bodily clock was running backwards, how little it could tell me of its troubles. It—Body—had always been a stranger. I'd never become acquainted with myself. And now, I felt, life itself depended upon communication.

Though Body was going back to its ancestors, *I* had things planned and underway. I was working on a screenplay that could be an important contribution to my ethnic group, the Mormons. A quarterly had requested an article on a vital subject. A novel was simmering. . . There were the best of reasons for establishing rapport with Body, combining with it to repel the enemy. But *how?*

The local library had an entire shelf under the heading of "Self," and as I read about the psyche and the unconscious I was impressed by the importance of self-knowledge and the rewards of exploring our own souls—yet I found no hint as to how this might be done, on a practical basis. How could I come to know the stranger I knew only in the mirror, "the individual human being" Jung called it in his *The Undiscovered Self*—"that infinitesimal unit on whom a world depends, and in whom, if we read the meaning of the Christian message aright, even God seeks his goal."

I'd thought I'd known the answers. Each and every day, without exception, I had made sure of exercise: golf three times a week, a stiff walk other days, and a session with the skip-rope every evening. At the clinic the doctors marveled at the strength and vitality with which my body fought the unknown enemy. Yet as the tests went on, the enemy was slowly winning. My brisk pace slowed to a shuffle and my deep voice became a high-pitched tremor.

With the bodily clock beginning to run backwards instead of feeling good after exercise, I felt terrible. The climax came on a lovely February afternoon when I played just twelve holes of golf, taking it easy, which caused my hands, wrists, ankles and feet to swell and remain that way. *All right, Body, we'll leave golf alone for awhile*, I said, and I wondered about other exercise that now seemed to pump poison through me instead of health. If I skipped rope, would it do to my heart what golf had done to my extremities?

The secret of all knowledge, the ancient Greeks said, was contained in two words: Know thyself. And our Bible tells us that the Kingdom of God is within us. How little I knew Body! I had fed it, clothed it, washed and sheltered it, not particularly for Body's benefit but my own. I had abused Body dreadfully, perverting its normal appetite through my indulgence in rich foods then subjecting it to a furious exercise and dieting program to avoid its becoming overweight.

I had considered myself hard as nails, and it was with curious detachment that I noted the shrinkage of vitality. Strength left arms and legs. I could no longer squat without falling. It became a challenge to depress the button of my automobile door to open it. Turning the key in the ignition was a distinct effort. It took both thumbs to squeeze the toothpaste tube. After a fall when I went down heavily I knew that Body was ready for a cane; but I didn't get one because *I* wasn't.

"Tell me," I asked of the stranger in the mirror, as I shaved the face of John Taylor, "what can I do to help you in this fight?"

No answer. Know thyself—how deep and difficult! Yet now, at last, I was trying. Though it might be too late, as Body day by day prepared itself for eternity, I was trying to understand it, to establish communication. Since babyhood, bodily impulses had been suppressed, directed, trained. Appetite of the infant was conditioned to a time schedule. Toilet training involved a long process of controlling natural impulse. "Children—*no running*!" came a voice over the din at supervised recreation, yet what is more natural than running? I was born a little animal who must be civilized, "conquered" was the term of an earlier day. Every bodily impulse must in some way be thwarted, diverted, trained, or ignored. The animal nature was bad, and this was particularly true of the sex drive, which made puberty a time of struggle, frustration, guilt, and horror. By the time I was an adult, virtually all communication between me and Body had been severed.

Appetite was habit, not hunger. Fatigue was circumvented by stimulants. Pain, as a warning signal, was ignored. I was tough, and took pride in not being a baby. I told my dentist he needn't deaden a tooth before drilling it. When struck with influenza at a time I was preparing to travel a thousand miles to deliver a speech, I made the trip and the talk as a matter of course, though so sick I had to cling to the lectern to steady myself. Hard as nails; tough it out; yeah, tiger!

But when the bodily clock began running backwards, when exercise brought penalties, not health, when all answers of a lifetime were wrong, I tried very hard to get through to Body, to make contact with my inner self. As I asked, "What can I do to help?" to the stranger in the mirror, Body made no reply. I had ignored, diverted, and thwarted natural impulse too many years.

As the clinic took more and more tests, there was a certain frantic urgency about it. I knew they were guessing wildly now, snatching at one thing and another, trying to find and locate the enemy before it was too late. Instead of two or three tests each week, there might be eight or ten. There was a morning when with a dozen others I took a routine blood test; then just two of us stayed for an extra one involving the injection of dye in a vein. As the woman who also took this test limped from the room, the nurse watched with tragic compassion and breathed, "Poor thing." Then the nurse turned to me with her professional smile. I knew the other woman was dying, and I was about to take the same test.

The clinic didn't know, so between visits there I went to a healer, not a medical doctor. What could it hurt? As I lay supine he folded his hands on my bare belly and closed his eyes. I closed mine, also, to help if possible. When he opened his eyes he said, "Your condition is your body's rebellion over mistreatment."

"All right. What do I do?" I wanted to know. I followed his instructions faithfully for a week, but was worse on my return, and he washed his hands of me by recommending a healer in another state. A friend of mine had had good results from another healer, so I tried him, but this man was afraid to touch me because the clinic had been unable to make a diagnosis.

These rejections were severe blows. I couldn't even get treated by people who make a living from the hopeless. I wondered if, as I shuffled from the clinic laboratory after the dye test, the nurse had murmured, "Poor fellow." Did they know, really, and weren't telling me?

Thursday at the clinic meant the usual wait. I'd gotten into the habit of taking a manuscript along, and I spent a profitable two hours on the screenplay before I finally got in to see the specialist. He leafed through the latest test results in my folder, face grave. Sick as I was, I smiled at the difference between the new and old practice of medicine. After the preliminary examination, a clinic doctor hardly glanced at the patient. The tests were everything. When I was first assigned to the specialist he said, "Now, I want to have a good, long talk with you about your condition," whereupon he picked up my folder, sat down to look it over, and never said another word.

And now after all the testing he sat thumbing the test slips and still had nothing to say.

"Well, how about it?" I asked him. "How bad is it?"

He forced a brief smile and without looking up from the folder said, "These are only pieces of paper, after all."

"Then the tests are bad?"

"Oh, things might go wrong in the testing," he said with an effort at heartiness. "Some slip-up, perhaps. We're not going to get discouraged over a few slips of paper, are we?"

Then he began making out forms for more tests, this time the whole works, a handful of slips. "You won't be able to arrange for all of these right away. So come in—let's see—four weeks from today." His voice trailed off, as if he'd been going to say something else. Our eyes met for a moment, then I took the handful of slips and went out. I thought I knew why his voice had trailed away; he wasn't sure I'd still be around in four weeks.

After making arrangements for the tests I took a walk. Every step was an effort. I fought to walk erect rather than stooped, prepared to fall. I knew that "rest"—inaction—meant death. I couldn't let John Taylor go to bed, or he never would get out of it. If I gave Body a cane, I could never take it away again.

I drove home that bleak Thursday afternoon and went out back to the little shack where I do my writing. I was worn out from the emotional ordeal and the walk, and stretched out on the couch for a few minutes. Such rests, I'd found, could carry me through the worst days. I'd never quit working every day, though there had been days when I must confess that I didn't get much done.

If I've got only another four weeks, or less, why am I lying here? I struggled off the studio couch stiffly and to the typewriter. Then I realized with horror that I'd left the script at the clinic. This screenplay was, in a way, the most important thing I'd ever written; we were trying to present, for the very first time, the Mormons as they really were, the Peculiar People. And I'd lost the original draft and only copy. If I didn't find it, I doubted if I'd have time or energy to re-create it over again.

At the clinic, nobody remembered the script in its red binder. It wasn't in the waiting room, nor in the room where I'd seen the specialist. No nurse had tucked it away. It was gone.

I was utterly discouraged as I drove home. I could never find the time nor energy to do that script over again from scratch. I wouldn't be able to write that article for the quarterly. The novel I had simmering, the play I was going to do someday. . . well, wasn't all life like this, ending in defeat?

A car was waiting when I arrived home, and out of it stepped a man with that red script binder in his hand.

"Your name was on it," he said, as I thanked him. "Hope you don't mind me reading it, but once I got started I couldn't stop."

"Sweet words to an author's ears."

"And I wanted to meet you," he said. "I knew you'd be such an interesting person."

An author is always embarrassed when confronted with the demand that he be interesting, and I'm afraid that this man, to whom I owed so much and whose name I never knew, was greatly disappointed, because I was literally stricken dumb by what he had said. Inside of me, a light had turned on; there was a dazzling insight to my problem. As he handed me the red binder I realized that the answer I had been so desperately searching for was lying right there on the pages of the script.

How many times over how many years had I spoken at writers' conventions, to women's clubs, and groups interested in the art of writing? They all wanted to know the secret. I had even taught a class in professional writing one winter at the adult night school. In these talks and at the class I had stressed, time and again, that good writing wasn't a matter of grammar, punctuation, or style. "What you have to offer, and all you'll ever sell, is *yourself*," I'd told them. "You are a unique person, and to be good your writing must have your own spark of life and your own heartbeat."

This was self-evident in the work of author friends. Each of them left his portrait in every single thing he wrote. Reading a book by a friend was like a personal visit.

I treasured the work of friends who had died, for their heart beat on in what they had left behind.

" . . . *such an interesting person.*"

I found that person in that script—and I must admit it *was* interesting to meet myself for the first time, the real me, the me that welled up from inside past the toilet training and sexual repression and dietary violation and tough-guy conquest of the animal body. Here was the clue to that in which the ancient Greeks placed such store, Know thyself. Here was the microcosm reflecting the great cosmos in miniature, which Christianity called the Kingdom of God within us.

Now I knew Body. Now I knew Me. "We'll work together," I told the face of John Taylor in the mirror. "Without a diagnosis, the clinic can't help us. We've got to do this alone."

Body told me, now that I could listen, the worth of an attribute which had been utterly foreign to what I had supposed to be my nature, moderation. With moderate exercise, moderate diet, moderate work habits, and moderate rest periods, we confronted the unknown enemy. Meanwhile I finished the screenplay, wrote the article for the quarterly, began taking notes on the novel.

After four weeks I was again with the specialist as he leafed through the results of the last batch of tests, never looking at me or asking how I felt.

"Say, you're getting better!" he exclaimed. "We're sure now that it's nothing *big*, and you'll get over what you've got, whatever it is."

This was no news to me. I had noticed the change in that face I shaved in the mirror, as day by day the deep-set eyes of John Taylor gave way to the full-lidded gaze of Samuel Woolley. Now I was again shaving the familiar countenance I'd known all my life but had come to understand only recently.

While I am sure that it would be too much to claim that meeting myself was the key to recovery, I think it is reasonable to assume that a whole man can fight better than a divided one. And I have wondered about other creative fields, such as painting, music, architecture—and wondered where creativity ceased. Do all of us leave evidence of our true selves in some aspect of our lives? Certainly cooking is an art; could a housewife find herself in an apple pie? But that is for the psychologists and philosophers. It was sufficient that I had found my own way, as each of us must. And whatever else, it had been worth walking in the shadow of death, if that were necessary for me, to experience one of life's great adventures in meeting myself.

I have lived thirty-five years beyond the predictions of the MDs. I have spent the time advancing my career. But in the meantime, and probably more important to my comfort and joy now, the family has grown, as well. My daughter and son-in-law still live next door and have presented us with two grandchildren. Patrick is a computer genius. He is twenty years old and a junior at Stanford. My cute little granddaughter, Elizabeth, is a junior in high school and keeps busy distinguishing herself by singing in two choirs, starring in the yearly community theatre musical productions, and giving several hours a week to Project Read. Last spring she won an essay contest which carried a thousand-dollar prize. Gay says her award at BYU was ten dollars.

The family went with me to Hawaii when I had to give a speech for the Mormon History Association five years ago. My wife and daughter attended speeches with me during the day, while Paul and the children saw the sights. At night we were entertained with singing, dancing and plays. It was a memorable vacation bringing together the two things that have made up my entire life, my writing and my family.

When I now look in the mirror, I am satisfied.